PAUL NEWMAN

PAUL NEWMAN

A Pyramid Illustrated History of the Movies

Copyright © 1974 by Pyramid Communications, Inc.

ISBN 0-515-03418-5

Library of Congress Catalog Card Number: 73-21126

Printed in the United States of America

Pyramid Books are published by Pyramid Communications, Inc. Its trademarks, consisting of the word "Pyramid" and the portrayal of a pyramid, are registered in the United States Patent Office.

Pyramid Communications, Inc.
919 Third Avenue, New York, N.Y. 10022

graphic design by anthony basile

To my mother and father

ACKNOWLEDGMENTS

I should like to thank the following for permitting me to screen films: Walter Dauler and Beatrice Herrmann of *Macmillan Audio Brandon,* Patricia Moore of *United Artists 16.*

I gratefully acknowledge the assistance and encouragement of the following: Thomas P. Allen, Warren and Anna Bass, Joanne D'Antonio, Robert Edelstein, Susan Gwertzman, Stephen Harvey, Foster Hirsch, William Kenly, Irving Werner, Seth Willenson, and my editor, Ted Sennett.

Finally, a special word of thanks to Charles Silver, for his inexhaustible patience in answering questions, and for the invaluable education he has given me in understanding movies.

Photographs from the collection of Jerry Vermilye, and from United Press International Photo.

CONTENTS

In 1959, Paul Newman was appearing on Broadway in Tennessee Williams' play, *Sweet Bird of Youth*. At a particularly intense moment of one matinee performance, a matron in the front row loudly remarked: "Hasn't he got the *bluest* eyes!"

The observation may have been out of place, but it was completely accurate. Newman's eyes are a strikingly bright blue (though, ironically, they are also color-blind). They are seemingly lit from within, and, in the words of a columnist, look as if they had "just finished taking a shower." Of course, they are more than merely beautiful —their hard, icy quality has frequently been used to imply a cold character—but many fans refuse to look for such nuances.

Naturally, this superficial appreciation has annoyed Newman: "If blue eyes are what it's all about, and not the accumulation of my work as a professional actor, I may as well go into gardening." He has also said, "I'd like to think that I could have been a successful actor if I'd had brown eyes."

On the record of his two decades of performances, Paul Newman would have to be judged an extremely successful actor. From what some thought to be a mere imitation of Brando in the fifties, he quickly developed into an actor who

A MAN OF MANY PARADOXES

could convey subtle layers of meaning and emotion, even in less than meaningful roles. Over the years he has matured into a man of many paradoxes, off-screen and on, an individual not susceptible of easy analysis, a complex personality masked by a deceptive facade.

To uncover the personality, one cannot avoid the externals. Whether he likes it or not, Newman is the quintessential matinee idol. Among the handsomest men in Hollywood's history, he suggests a Greek statue, with his classic profile and sensual mouth (as well as those ethereal eyes). And even though Newman wants to be considered exclusively on the basis of acting ability, he realizes that much of his success is due to good looks. In fact, almost as if to negate this, he likes to disguise himself. In private, he often wears dark glasses, a cap pulled down over his forehead, and a scruffy beard. Two of his favorite films are *Hemingway's Adventures of a Young Man* and *The Outrage*, and in both he was almost unrecognizable. For *The Prize* and *Lady L* he wanted to grow a beard, but MGM refused, thinking that it would ruin his image.

Newman's somewhat whimsical wish to look more "ordinary" is part of a serious desire to deny his superstar status. Today it's not unusual for stars to turn their backs on the traditional Hollywood trappings —the huge mansion, mink bedspread, personal appearance tours, premieres, interviews, autograph parties—but Newman has, from the start of his career in 1954, refused to go along with "that fraud." He has lived far from Hollywood (since the early sixties, in Westport, Connecticut), dressed informally, expressed his opinions on political issues before speaking out was fashionable, and constantly rebelled against traditional advice. For example, although a big star was not supposed to take small parts, he did so in the Hemingway film, mainly because he liked the character. In addition, he has returned to the stage to take chances in front of audiences, and, at the height of his box-office popularity, he temporarily left acting to begin a new career as a director. To the chagrin of gossip columnists, he has also insisted on keeping his private life private. He gives the appearance of being an everyday, normal family man whose occupation happens to be movie star.

Another paradox is that Newman, who has been acting professionally for over two decades, claims he doesn't enjoy acting. For him, it requires an enormous amount of work and self-discipline. His training in the Stanislavski Method as interpreted by Lee Strasberg at the Actors Studio has led him to examine motivations and meanings, and to consider every role "a study session." He likes to draw distinctions between an instinctive performer, like his wife, Joanne Woodward, and a "cerebral" actor, like himself: "Some people are born intuitive actors and have . . . the talent to slip in and out of the characters they are creating . . . Acting to me is like dredging a river. It's a painful experience. I simply do not have the intuitive talent. I worry about acting and constantly complain to myself about my own performances."*

The drive for perfection has caused Newman to immerse himself completely in his characters. He learned to play the trombone for *Paris Blues,* perfected his pool game for *The Hustler,* did some riding and went on a roundup before making *The Left-Handed Gun,* lived on an Indian reservation before making *Hombre* and in a bunkhouse before filming *Hud.* He has often visited locations well in advance, in order to study local customs and speech patterns, and he likes to rehearse for two weeks before shooting.

*John Ferris, "Acting is a Painful Experience," *New York World Telegram and Sun,* September 12, 1959.

This is all characteristic of the Method, as is his desire to go against the tradition of personality actors like Cagney, Gable, Cooper and Wayne, who were often said to be "playing themselves." He has stated his wish to avoid going from one "Paul Newman role" to another. Yet, ironically, for twenty years he has been creating variations on a single, clearly identifiable character. He may not be playing "himself"—that is, his real personality—but he *is* playing what has become a popular *image* of his personality. And this is precisely what has made him a star. All of the truly legendary actors and actresses stayed within the boundaries of easily recognizable images; it was permissible to depart occasionally, but they always had to return. Certainly Newman has given many strong performances, but in a relatively narrow range—one with which the public can easily connect.

This is not meant in the least as a denigration of Newman's talent, because very few actors have the ability to connect in this way. And even fewer can make their screen personalities dominate their films so completely. There is a distinctive feel to a Newman film, and it makes almost no difference what the subject is, or who directs it, or who writes it. Of course, as his career developed, films were written expressly with him in mind, and

therefore his image was carefully considered; others were transformed during shooting. Newman's influence extends to recurring lines, gestures, expressions, even positioning of actors.

In examining this distinctive Newman personality, one continues to find paradoxes. His screen image is generally the antithesis of his private personality. A "cerebral," intellectual actor, he has played many spontaneous, uninhibited men. Privately shy, insecure and nervous, he has portrayed quite a few cool, confident, and charming characters. For someone who hates references to his looks, he has played an amazing number of roles in which his good looks are emphasized; in film after film, for example, Newman is seen stripped to the waist, and his bare chest has become almost as prominent as his blue eyes.

Furthermore, Newman, who is committed passionately to humanitarian and liberal causes, has created a huge gallery of men who are basically committed to nothing except themselves. In reality he's a dedicated family man, with a successful marriage and six children, but in only one film, *Somebody Up There Likes Me*, is there what may be termed a happy marriage, and it's hardly an example of marital bliss. In only that film and two others—*Rally 'Round the Flag, Boys!* and *The Life and Times of*

Judge Roy Bean– does he have children, and none of these portray warm family relationships. Finally, in sharp contrast with his real-life devotion to one woman for over sixteen years, his characters are ladies' men who are invariably rough, rotten and ruthlessly exploitative. They are incapable of much tenderness, and seldom place women anywhere near a pedestal; instead, they rape them, insult them, use them, discard them like old rags, subordinate them entirely to ambition.

Ambition is, in fact, a key part of the Newman image. His characters usually possess it in overabundance. Some are born on the wrong side of the tracks, and desire wealth and its attendant status. Others are not necessarily interested in money—the goal may be winning a pool game or an auto race, or carrying through a mission, but the means are the same. These men usually set aside considerations of love, family, humanity, and morality, and they push forward ruthlessly. The are arrogant, conceited, selfish and irresponsible, which inevitably alienates them from friends and society.

Yet we rarely see them in simple terms of good and evil. Sometimes the script endows them with likable traits, but generally it is Newman's performance that enables us to identify with many of his most selfish characters' problems and obsessions. These nasty men have the saving grace of being aware of their own nastiness and turning it into charm. Newman has continually projected boyishness, good will and a sense of humor, which make him attractive and engaging. It cannot be avoided that much of our sympathy is generated by Newman's looks. He may portray obnoxious, aggressive, rough, virile types, but his features suggest intelligence and sensitivity. Occasionally this works against the film's intention, making him less a villain than he is supposed to be, but it's difficult to be alienated completely from the handsome all-American boy.

Newman's characters also evoke sympathy by the extreme loneliness to which they are invariably brought. A typical protagonist is withdrawn into his own world, and builds a protective shell around himself. Although that shell hurts people who try to come close, it also makes him a pathetically isolated man. In addition, he's often a sad, hopeless alcoholic. A characteristic scene has him holding a beer can, producing a hidden flask, drinking cheap whiskey, or staring intently at a glass of liquor and holding it as if it were part of his body.

He's further humanized by his susceptibility to extreme physical pain. For example, in *Somebody Up There Likes Me*, *Harper* and *The Mackintosh Man* he's severely

beaten; in *The Hustler* his thumbs are broken; in *Sweet Bird of Youth* his face is smashed; in *The Left-Handed Gun* he crashes through a window to escape a fire; in *Judge Roy Bean* he's dragged from a horse with a rope tied around his neck; in *Cat on a Hot Tin Roof* he hobbles around with a broken ankle; in *Cool Hand Luke* he's continually beaten and tortured. This appeals to Newman partly because it sometimes renders him temporarily ugly, but the severe degradation and pain also create an atmosphere of vulnerability that facilitates audience identification.

Finally, Newman's anti-heroes have been embraced especially by young audiences because they symbolize the general alienation and rebellion of youth in the fifties and sixties. He began, with films like *Somebody Up There Likes Me* and *The Left-Handed Gun*, in the tradition established by fellow Actors Studio alumni Marlon Brando and James Dean—that of the confused, inarticulate rebel who knows only that he must strike out at the world, but cannot explain why. But the image soon changed into that of a rebel who is relatively intelligent, more in control of himself, better able to define his cause: a thinking man's rebel. The Hustler, Chance Wayne *(Sweet Bird of Youth)* and Hud can describe what makes them tick, and although they are certainly not interested in bettering society, their very ability to articulate made them connect with sixties youth.

In the late sixties, with characters like Hombre and Cool Hand Luke, Newman returned to the silent rebels, but with a difference. Now they *choose* to remain silent: they are not confused or directionless, but are intelligent individuals who elect to separate themselves from humanity. They have no definite goals, but become loners because it's the only way they can survive.

Their ending up as martyrs is irrelevant, because it happens almost against their will—as a gratuitous act that defines them as modern, existential rebels. And, at least in the case of Luke, audiences could easily identify with the rebellion.

In the seventies, Newman has been playing right-wing types, like Hank Stamper in *Sometimes a Great Notion* and Judge Roy Bean; or complete mercenaries without ideals, like Rheinhardt in *WUSA* and Rearden in *The Mackintosh Man*, whose dedication to survival becomes extreme. Their life styles and philosophies are antithetical not only to Newman's, but to those of seventies youth, which may be a reason Newman has been losing his audience.

But for over a decade, he was our most important film actor. He filled a vacuum created by the death of Dean and the subsequent decline of Clift and Brando—the three most important actors to emerge in the fifties. But Newman did not win only by default—there were certainly other new actors around. He ascended to prominence because he was able to embody best the rebellion and dissatisfactions of his era, while possessing a classic handsomeness that his contemporaries lacked. He was at once the perfect modern anti-hero and the link with a glamorous Hollywood that was rapidly fading into memory.

Paul Newman never had an overwhelming ambition to be an actor; as he puts it, he "backed into" the profession. In fact, he almost spent his life selling baseball gloves, or, at best, teaching theatre history and criticism in Ohio.

The characters he often plays —angry young men from the wrong side of town or rebellious loners —have little in common with the young Newman. The setting is Shaker Heights, Ohio, a fashionable suburb about eight miles from Cleveland—a serene, beautifully landscaped area with private homes, gardens and upper-middle-class families. It was into this comfortable environment that Paul Newman was born on January 26, 1925. His parents were second-generation Americans: Arthur, from a German-Jewish family; Theresa (Fetzer), from a Hungarian- Roman Catholic family. His mother left the Church when Paul was young, and for some reason he was raised as a Christian Scientist, which he says "didn't really take on me." The family was well off—Arthur owned an extremely successful sporting goods store in Cleveland, reputedly one of the largest in the country—and Paul grew up in a spacious, eleven-room house.

If Newman successfully combines virility and sensitivity, perhaps the origin lies in the con-

FROM SHAKER HEIGHTS TO BROADWAY

flicting parental influences. As a boy he was interested, as was his father, in sports; but his mother, who Newman once said might have been a frustrated actress, wanted him to act. He joined "The Curtain Raisers," the children's group in the Cleveland community theatre. At age eight he was a court jester in *The Travails of Robin Hood,* in which he performed a yodel solo composed by his uncle Joe Newman, a journalist and poet. At twelve he had his first starring role, as St. George. He also continued to pursue sports, and at Shaker Heights High School, he excelled at football, basketball and baseball. Not surprisingly, sports are prominent in a number of his films. (A photo of the young Newman with a football is even used in *Cat on a Hot Tin Roof.*)

On graduation in 1942 he enrolled at Kenyon College, Gambier, Ohio, but in 1943 he enlisted in the Navy. He was assigned to the V-12 education program but was dropped four months later for color blindness. During the following two years he served as a radioman-gunner on naval torpedo planes in Okinawa and Guam, but saw little combat. In 1946 he returned to Kenyon, on the G.I. Bill, and majored in economics. Newman attributes his becoming involved in dramatics to an incident at the start of his junior year, when some brawling led him to spend the night in jail and to be thrown off the football team. With the unexpected free time, he decided to read for a play. Over the next two years he did ten plays, and even directed and starred in a musical.

Newman has said that he acted because it was the only way he had of getting attention, but that it was a painful process: "You have to learn to take off your clothes emotionally on stage. I was lousy. I couldn't let go, yet I wanted to act." He graduated with a Bachelor of Science degree in 1949. According to Newman, Kenyon graduated him "magna cum kindness of their hearts;" he insists that the yearbook actually says he was graduated "magnum cum lager." (The college did think enough of him to award him an honorary degree, Doctor of Humane Letters, in 1962.)

Immediately after graduation, he joined a summer repertory company in Williams Bay, Wisconsin, where he appeared in *The Glass Menagerie, Suspect* and *The Candlestick Maker*. That fall he joined the Woodstock (Illinois) Players, and performed in sixteen plays, including *Cyrano de Bergerac, Icebound* and *Dark of the Moon*.

While starring in *John Loves Mary,* he met Jackie Witte, an attractive member of the company. Shortly thereafter, in December, 1949, they were married. (The marriage lasted until 1956, and they had three children: Scott, born 1951; Susan, born 1953; and Stephanie, born 1954.)

Soon after Newman's wedding, his father died, and he interrupted his career to return home and manage the store. But after almost two years, in 1951, he turned the business over to his brother, and left to attend the prestigious Yale Drama School: "Out of no burning desire to act, but to flee from the store. All this crap about grease paint! And after Yale I didn't have stars in my eyes. I knew what this rat race was. I wanted a Master's Degree because my dream was to return to Kenyon and teach. I just fell into acting." At Yale he received some attention for a play in which he portrayed Beethoven's nephew. Encouraged by his instructors, he left Yale in the summer of 1952 for New York. If he didn't succeed, he would return to school in the fall.

Newman never returned, his goal of an academic life gone forever. His was by no means the traditional painful struggle toward success; as he has often said, "I was very, very lucky." The breaks came rapidly, and in a short time he was appearing regularly on television, on such shows as *The Web, You Are There,*

Danger, and *The Mask.* By September he had a running part in *The Aldrich Family* at the princely salary of $200 a month. Then, in November, he was cast in the Broadway production of William Inge's *Picnic.*

He had wanted to play the leading character, Hal Carter, but director Joshua Logan cast Ralph Meeker. Newman would have been perfect as Hal, a wanderer who disrupts the quiet of a small town and awakens the emotions of a number of women. Hal possessed the virility, sense of freedom and romance, and air of self-assurance that Newman would bring to many of his film roles; he was, in fact, strikingly similar to Ben Quick in *The Long Hot Summer.* But Newman had to be content with the somewhat different role of Alan Seymour, a shy, conventional Princeton boy who places women on a pedestal, and who loses his girl to Hal.

Nonetheless, *Picnic* was an extraordinary break; just six months out of Yale, he was in a major Broadway play. It opened on February 19, 1953, and Newman received good reviews; Brooks Atkinson in *The New York Times* said, "Paul Newman as a college lad infatuated with pretty faces . . . (helps) to bring to life all the cross-currents of Mr. Inge's sensitive writing." *Picnic* was very successful, running for fourteen months and winning the Pulitzer Prize. Newman understudied Meeker, and got to play the lead for two weeks. He also met and became attracted to a young Southern actress named Joanne Woodward, who was understudying several female roles.

The financial security provided by a steady job enabled him to expand artistically. He began to study at the Actors Studio, which he considers "the best training ground for young actors in America . . . they've got to take the accolade or blame for whatever it is I've become as an actor." During *Picnic*'s run he studied under Lee Strasberg and Elia Kazan, and learned from observing his contemporaries at the studio: Geraldine Page, Kim Stanley, Eli Wallach, Anne Jackson, and a young man who would later haunt his career—James Dean.

His star was steadily rising. *Theatre World* picked him (along with Page) as one of 1953's "Promising Personalities." ·More importantly, he was noticed by Warner Brothers, who offered him a seven-year contract. Newman decided to leave *Picnic* prior to its national tour. He was now in his thirtieth year—a crucial time in anyone's life, when it seems that one should be established in a career or face a severe crisis of self-confidence. During that important spring of 1954, Paul Newman was packing his bags and heading for Hollywood.

The sweet smell of success quickly turned sour: as soon as he arrived at Warners, Newman was hurried into a bizarre religious epic, *The Silver Chalice* (1954). Based on a recent best-seller by Thomas B. Costain, and directed by Victor Saville, who was fresh from a Mickey Spillane movie, this $4½-million, overlong costume drama was sub-Spillane in its writing and sub-DeMille in its spectacle. It was one of the studio's early CinemaScope films, and was really a variation on Fox's *The Robe*, the first CinemaScope movie that had been a huge success in 1953. The action follows a group of Christians who are dedicated to preserving Christ's Holy Cup twenty years after the Last Supper. The religious theme becomes an excuse for adventure, romance and typical Hollywood pseudo-piety, with absurd dialogue, ludicrous costumes, and oddly stylized stage sets that made the film unintentionally avant-garde. All of this prompted one critic to remark, "There are moments of which the Marx Brothers would be proud, especially Groucho."

Since Newman had the lead, he was spared the necessity of working his way up through supporting roles, but it was a mixed blessing. A young Greek silversmith, he is sold into slavery, is chosen by the Christians to design a chalice for the Cup, becomes involved in battles and or-

THE SHADOWS OF BRANDO AND DEAN

gies, and must choose between the pagan world represented by a courtesan (Virginia Mayo) and the Christian world represented by his young, innocent wife (Pier Angeli). There's also a mad pagan magician (Jack Palance), who wants to destroy the chalice and establish his own religion, replacing Christ's miracles with black magic. In the climax, Palance tries to prove he's a god by attempting to fly!

Warners, undoubtedly hoping for the critics' good will toward men, opened this disaster on Christmas Day, 1954, but no one brought tidings of joy. It was universally panned, as was Newman, who displays some virility in the role, but is generally as bad as the material. The *New Yorker* critic quipped: "Paul Newman delivers his lines with the emotional fervor of a conductor announcing local stops." Of course, Newman was ideally cast as a Greek, because of his classic features, but it was a different resemblance that virtually everyone noticed. *The New York World Telegram* referred to him as "a new boy, Jack (sic) Newman, who bears an astonishing resemblance to Marlon Brando, an excessively sullen Marlon." And so it went, with Newman

THE SILVER CHALICE (1954). As Basil.

THE SILVER CHALICE (1954). With Virginia Mayo.

being called a "blond Brando," "cut-rate Brando," "imitation Brando."

This is certainly not new in movies; as Newman himself has said, "It never fails. Sooner or later every newcomer to Hollywood is told he is 'another somebody or other'." But Newman was making his film debut at a particularly unfortunate time. 1954 was the year of *The Wild One* and *On the Waterfront,* and Brando was at the height of his popularity; his fervent admirers were wary of the many imitators—the moody, rebellious, Actors Studio types who were infiltrating Hollywood. At the opposite extreme, there were many Brando jokes, and to some, "another Brando" meant another mumbler to avoid. Newman has always been justifiably angry at what he calls "lazy journalism"—analyzing actors on the basis of looks—and his desire to be considered only for his talent must have originated in this early, unpleasant experience. He remained sensitive about the Brando label, which people kept putting on him until as late as 1958.

The Silver Chalice almost destroyed Newman's film career at its beginning, and today he views it as "the worst film to be made in the entirety of the fifties," and a considerable embarrassment. When it was scheduled for an entire week on Los Angeles television, he took out a newspaper ad. Bordered by a black

24

memorial wreath, it stated: "Paul Newman apologizes every night this week—Channel 9." Naturally, this only aroused curiosity, and the film got some of the highest ratings in L.A. television history. Newman says: "I didn't know what to do. It was all meant as a joke. A rather expensive one, but quite fun."*

In 1954 he was somewhat less amused. After one look at the film he wired his agent: "Get me back on Broadway." Like Bette Davis in earlier days, he rebelled against Warners, deciding that he must take charge of his career. Otherwise he might constantly be getting roles in which his looks and physique would be exploited and his acting ability ignored. Thus, despite his contract, he left Hollywood, determined not to return until he was either financially independent or artistically reputable enough to choose his roles. At least he knew he would never make another costume picture.

Again he was lucky, for on February 18, 1955, less than two months after *The Silver Chalice* had opened, he *was* back on Broadway, in a play that probably saved his career: Joseph Hayes' suspense drama, *The Desperate Hours*. As Glenn Griffin, the ruthless, psychotic leader of a group of prison escapees who terrorize an average

*Robin Bean, "Success Begins at Forty," *Films and Filming*, January 1966, p. 8.

American family, Newman stole the show. He liked the play, because he was cast against type, in what was really a Bogart role: although there was less philosophizing and more tension, it was reminiscent of *The Petrified Forest*. The director, Robert Montgomery, deliberately chose him because of his looks, believing that the villain would be even more frightening if he were a clean-cut youth. (The film of *The Desperate Hours*, more conventionally, cast Bogart in the role.) This began an image—the Adonis as villain—that Newman would continue to project. Another aspect of the play would recur in his films: the young man who takes out his father-hatred on the world.

The play received enthusiastic reviews; John Chapman of *The New York Daily News* said, "The major performance . . . is that of Paul Newman . . . it is evil, neurotic and vibrant—a first-class piece of work . . . there could be no more stir-crazy and animal-crafty desperado . . . a splendid, tensely maniacal performance." By March, Newman was elevated to co-star billing, and began to develop the kind of adulation that has continued uninterrupted ever since. There were teenage girls who had reportedly seen the play a dozen times, and who waited nightly at the stage door.

The Desperate Hours ran for six

THE DESPERATE HOURS (1955). With Karl Malden and Nancy Coleman.

months—until August 16th— during which Newman went to the Actors Studio twice a week, and continued pursuing television roles. A month after he completed his run as the demented killer, he went to the opposite extreme, starring as a wholesome, seventeen-year-old high school student in an NBC musical version of *Our Town*. It featured Frank Sinatra as narrator and co-starred Eva Marie Saint, who had recently won an Oscar for *On The Waterfront*. Newman's appearance with a former Brando co-star again brought up the Brando comparison (as, indeed, had his co-starring with Karl Malden in *The Desperate Hours*).

But it was someone else who would haunt Newman's career. On September 30, 1955, James Dean was killed in an automobile accident, shortly before he was to play Hemingway's *The Battler* in a television adaptation. Newman, who was supposed to co-star as the youth, Nick Adams, was persuaded to step in and take over the Dean role, that of a "pulp-faced, brainless old bum." The show, produced on NBC in October, and directed by Arthur Penn, showed the boxer as a brash and unbeatable champion at twenty, an incorrigible tough guy in prison at thirty, and a punch-drunk panhandler at forty. Since the one-hour show was live, Newman had to

THE RACK (1956). With Anne Francis.

undergo some quick make-up changes, which eventually turned him into an unrecognizable, ugly man—with cauliflower ears, flattened nose, misshapen mouth and half-closed eyes. He was so fond of the role that he recreated it in 1962 for *Hemingway's Adventures of a Young Man.*

Dean's shadow extended further: watching the show that night were Robert Wise and Charles Schnee, who were planning to direct and produce, respectively, a film version of Rocky Graziano's autobiography, *Somebody Up There Likes Me,* which, ironically, had been scheduled for Dean. Newman impressed them, and once again he was called upon to replace Dean. Although he was still under contract at Warners, the studio agreed to loan him to MGM for the picture. Since it was a far cry from *The Silver Chalice,* and because production head Dore Schary personally took an interest in him, Newman returned to Hollywood in October.

Shooting was scheduled to begin in January, but in late 1955, Glenn Ford quit MGM's *The Rack,* and the studio hurried Newman into yet another inherited role. In this film, adapted by Stewart Stern from a Rod Serling television play, Newman is an Army captain who returns to the U.S. after having been a POW for over two years in Korea, and is promptly charged with col-laboration. Most of the film centers on his court-martial, which reveals that he did indeed cooperate with his captors after intensive psychological torture. Since he admits that he never reached the breaking point, he is found guilty, but the film suggests that society is responsible in not better preparing soldiers for the new methods of torture.

From the moment he first appears in a wheelchair to be interviewed by a psychiatrist (evoking memories of Brando in *The Men*), through intense scenes with his father (Walter Pidgeon), a cold, stern career officer, to the climactic confession, Newman projects the brooding, nervous, introverted quality of a man still in a state of emotional shock. Method mannerisms that Newman carries from film to film first appear here, and although sometimes overdone, they are generally effective: his glistening eyes, nervously moving lips and rapid blinking; his habits of rubbing his head, looking away from people and putting his hand over his mouth while speaking. All of these suggest a man burdened with guilt, withdrawn into his own world of shame and bitter memories.

Newman is at his best during the trial, when he describes the prison camp horrors. Staring straight ahead, he recites his experience in a cool, deliberate manner, to prevent

THE RACK (1956). With Edmond O'Brien and Wendell Corey.

himself from breaking down. But he finally cries when recounting the fear of loneliness that led him to give in—a fear that was born in his childhood, when his mother died and his father never had time for him. He cries out: "My father never kissed me!"

Thus ultimately the film's focus is the alienation between child and parent, which places it in the tradition of many mid-fifties films, including Dean's *Rebel Without a Cause* (also written by Stern) and *East of Eden*. That theme would continue in Newman's films: from *Somebody Up There Likes Me*, through *Cat on a Hot Tin Roof* and others, to *Hud*, he plays men with serious problems in relating to a father or father-figure. In that context, *The Rack*'s central scene, which follows the confession, has the father attempting a reconciliation. The two sit in a car, with Newman again staring straight ahead, maintaining the barrier between them. He stiffens as his father puts his arm around him, but finally gives in as the old man does kiss him. It's the film's most poignant moment—a personal victory for the soldier, who loses everywhere else.

MGM opened *The Rack* in several key cities, but withdrew it from national release: They decided that this downbeat film would do better if it were released after the Graziano story, which everyone sensed would make Newman a star. There was much studio ballyhoo over *Somebody Up There Likes Me*, with press releases claiming (inaccurately) that Newman had been cast after an eight-month search, and ads announcing: "MGM presents a most important motion picture." They gave Newman star billing, and hoped audiences would discover him.

With characteristic seriousness, Newman prepared for the role by spending a week with Graziano —studying his speech, gestures, walk and mannerisms. When the film opened, the Brando comparisons were more prevalent than ever, not only because of the physical resemblance, but because Newman sounded like the Brando of *On the Waterfront* (in which he too had played a boxer) and *A Streetcar Named Desire*. But Brando, who was a friend of Graziano's, had studied the fighter's walk and speech patterns before doing *Streetcar* on Broadway; thus Newman, who naturally also copied Graziano, was, ironically, thought to be imitating Brando!

Newman does succeed in capturing the familiar Graziano mannerisms: the crude, New York-Italian accent; the mumbling; the disgruntled sneers and pouts; the jaunty walk, with huddled shoulders and shuffling feet. He has a nervous energy, wiping his mouth and nose with his fingers, rubbing his hands together, scratching his neck, and dancing around in one place, as if constantly facing an opponent in the ring. This perpetual motion—even when he is seated —suggests a potentially explosive force that naturally finds release in fighting, and it contrasts with the generally listless movement of Brando and Dean. The role is tremendously showy, and it gives Newman a chance to play an extrovert, as contrasted with his character in *The Rack*. And whereas his soldier was an intelligent man, his Rocky is almost subhuman, a purely physical being.

Wise and scriptwriter Ernest Lehman sketch in Graziano's impoverished childhood in New York's East Side slums, where he grows up in the streets, among hoodlums and gangs. His father (Harold J. Stone), a disappointed, third-rate ex-boxer, takes out his frustrations by drinking and by beating up Rocky; his mother (Eileen Heckart), is an unhappy, nervous wreck. As a result, Rocky becomes a brutal delinquent, spending most of his youth in reformatories and prisons. Defiant, cocky, striking out with his fists at anyone, he is seemingly incorrigible. Even the Army can't tame him—he punches an officer, goes AWOL and is sentenced to hard labor—but in prison he learns that

SOMEBODY UP THERE LIKES ME (1956). With Pier Angeli.

he can turn his hatred into a living: instead of fighting the world he can punch one man at a time in the ring. He becomes a successful fighter, marries a devoted woman, Norma (Pier Angeli), and eventually makes it in the "legit" world, becoming middleweight champion.

The story is in the tradition of a number of fifties movies about delinquency and rebellion. Newman's portrayal of Rocky as an inarticulate teenager is similar to Brando's motorcyclist in *The Wild One*, who also rebels against anything handy. But unlike the Brando character, Rocky develops from a causeless rebel into someone with a clear goal—to become a respected member of society—and this strong ambition allies him with many of Newman's subsequent characters.

The parent-child relationships, while similar to those in films like *Rebel Without a Cause*, suggest other Newman films as well. In *The Rack*, Newman says he's "half my father's disappointment—half my mother's hope," and the situation here is the same. Alienated from his vicious father, he runs out "to be something," and strikes back at the world. Their final confrontation, in which each recognizes his responsibility toward, and need for, the other, is a powerful moment; and the two reaching awkwardly for each other recalls the car scene in *The Rack*. Another affecting scene is his mother's visit to him in prison, where she says he must help himself. This prefigures the mother-son

SOMEBODY UP THERE LIKES ME (1956). With Everett Sloane.

SOMEBODY UP THERE LIKES ME (1956). With Pier Angeli.

confrontation in *Cool Hand Luke*, except that in the latter, both realize that the rebel cannot change, whereas here there's hope that Rocky will "turn the leaf."

MGM had wanted to make Rocky more of a comical prankster, but Newman resisted: "You can't make anything threatening out of a buffoon. Rocky had to be more than a poor misunderstood kid. He had to be brutal because his only business was survival." Still, there are a number of scenes in which he appears almost as a clown, which succeed in taking the edge off his nerv-ousness and in making him more likable. Newman also effectively portrays Rocky's sincere but clumsy attempts at tenderness with Norma; in subsequent films he would play many men who have difficulty being tender (although usually they can put on an air of confidence, and are not so awkward). Rocky is made even more sympathetic by his genuine concern for a fellow hoodlum (Sal Mineo), whose idolatry of Rocky as a father-figure evokes the similar relationship between Mineo and Dean in *Rebel Without a Cause*.

Somebody Up There Likes Me opened in the summer of 1956 to rave reviews, with Newman especially praised; William K. Zinsser of *The New York Herald Tribune* predicted, "Newman . . . should jump to movie stardom with this role." His new status as a rising star made him especially eager to hold out for a good part at Warners. In the meantime he appeared in television dramas, playing a wide variety of roles. In *Bang the Drum Slowly* (made into a film in 1973) he was a baseball player who helps a dying teammate conceal his illness from the team; in *The Rag Jungle* he fought racketeers in the garment business; in *The Five Fathers of Pepi* he was one of five Italian merchants who care for an orphan boy.

The Rack finally opened in November, and Newman was singled out for praise. He returned to Warners early in 1957 and displayed a still-rebellious attitude. On the first day of shooting for his next film he had a photo taken of himself, emerging from a deep freeze, and sent it to studio head Jack L. Warner, along with a caption: "Paul Newman, who was kept in the deep freeze for two years because of *The Silver Chalice*, has at last been thawed out by Warner Brothers to play the cold-hearted gangster in *The Helen Morgan Story*." He also presented the director, Michael Curtiz, and the pro-

ducer with whips, "to be used on me—in case I get difficult."

One wonders why Newman chose to return for this film, a typical Hollywood "biography" that transforms an artist's life into a cliché-ridden soap opera. It explains the decline of Helen Morgan (Ann Blyth) into alcoholism as the result of unsuccessful romances, especially one with Larry Maddux (Newman), a two-bit bootlegger. Larry is an almost one-dimensional and ultimately unbelievable character, but he does have qualities that are developed further in later Newman films: he is opportunistic, exploitative, smooth-talking, a man from the wrong side of the tracks who tries to better himself. Like other Newman characters, he is an outlaw—a con man and gangster —and it is noteworthy that Curtiz had directed Cagney, Bogart and other tough guys in Warners' Golden Era. Larry is also the first of Newman's womanizers—detached, rough, abusive, but irresistibly charming and sexy. He manages to seduce Helen while remaining nasty and cynical, then abandons her, only to keep reappearing and ruining her life. At best he can say, "In my own way, Helen, I love you," although in the unconvincing ending, he reforms.

Neither *The Helen Morgan Story* nor Newman fared well with the critics, and he says he occasionally

THE HELEN MORGAN STORY (1957). With Ann Blyth.

tries to forget the film. In 1957 there was little time to reflect: the day after he finished it he started *Until They Sail*. Again he was at MGM, under director Robert Wise, and again this was a move for the better—although the film is another soggy soap opera. Adapted by Robert Anderson from one of James Michener's *Return to Paradise* stories, it opens with Newman, as a military officer, testifying at a trial, which reminds one of *The Rack*. Indeed the subject once more is the way people surrender their ideals and moral standards under the pressures of war. But here the emphasis is on *women,* and the story details the endless suffering and sacrifices of four sisters on the New Zealand homefront during World War II.

Newman, an American marine, becomes involved with one of the sisters (Jean Simmons), whose husband has recently been killed in combat. It's hardly a smooth relationship: Simmons doesn't trust the G.I.s, who exploit and abuse the local women; Newman, who has been, in his words, "recently unmarried," has no faith in women or in romance. He is withdrawn, sullen, defensive, and trying to remain detached; and he uses his position as investigator of servicemen's prospective brides to advise men against marriage.

This is the first of Newman's genuine alcoholics. When Simmons

UNTIL THEY SAIL (1957). With Jean Simmons.

UNTIL THEY SAIL (1957). With Jean Simmons.

first meets him, he's in a bar, preoccupied with his liquor, and later, when she asks him how he copes with life, he shows her a bottle and delivers what would become characteristic Newman lines: "This is what I spend the night with—and no regrets . . . And nobody gets hurt." Gradually this confused and cynical man is unable to resist Simmons, who, he realizes, is the only woman he's ever really liked. He abandons what she calls his "hot affair with the bottle," although they seem to avoid a sexual relationship. Some melodramatic events threaten to keep them apart, but all ends happily in a huge CinemaScope closeup embrace.

Newman manages to rise above the film's excessive suds and subplotting. Occasionally he relies on the familiar blinking, twitching, throat-clearing and nervous, averted looks, but he conveys a touching vulnerability. More than in most of his films, the character's hard-boiled, liquor-coated protective shell only barely masks his insecurities and neuroses. Instead of showing his usual aggressiveness with women, he becomes very dependent, seeing Simmons as almost a mother and letting her see his weaknesses. Most Newman characters are emotionally immature but they are seldom as open about it —seldom as overtly passive, dependent and adolescent.

However, in his next film, *The Left-Handed Gun* (1958), a portrait of Billy the Kid, he was the complete adolescent, and came closer than ever to playing a James Dean character. (In fact, although Newman had starred in the original Gore Vidal TV version, Dean had been interested in doing the film.) Newman once distinguished himself from Dean by citing the latter's "lost little boy's point of view," but that is precisely Newman's interpretation of Billy. An uneducated, confused, neurotic adolescent, his Billy has more in common with a fifties delinquent than with any traditional Western hero (such as the heroic, romantic outlaw played by Robert Taylor in 1941's *Billy the Kid*).

The anti-heroic, anti-romantic concept is at the heart of all of Newman's films set in the West. The antithesis of John Wayne and Gary Cooper, he never plays conventional cowboys or lawmen, choosing instead notorious types (Butch Cassidy, Judge Roy Bean), outcasts (Carrasco in *The Outrage*, Hombre) or modern anti-heroic Westerners (Hud, Kane in *Pocket Money*)—deviants from normal Western society, with their own standards of justice and morality. The psychology of the outcast is also a preoccupation of director Arthur Penn, who made his film debut with *The Left-Handed Gun*, and who continued portraying outsiders in

THE LEFT-HANDED GUN (1958). Billy the Kid in town.

films like *Bonnie and Clyde, Alice's Restaurant* and *Little Big Man*. From the opening scene, in which Billy emerges from the horizon, a struggling, lone wanderer, his separateness from others is constantly stressed. Like other Newman protagonists, he's a man (or boy) drawn into himself, an island of introversion largely separated from humanity.

Penn is also known for his skill at conveying character and psychological states through physical gestures and movement, and here too he is well-allied with Newman (and with the Method). Billy is fairly inarticulate, bewildered, sometimes almost half-witted, in his speech, and animal-like in his movements (in this he resembles Rocky). Emotionally frustrated, inwardly directed, struggling to release his feelings, Billy "speaks" in terms of heightened physical action—intense facial expressions, broad gestures, extensive body movements—culminating in violence. Unlike Rocky, who learns to channel his instinct for violence into an acceptable outlet, Billy can only kill.

Characters like Rocky and Hud rebel because of father-hatred, but Billy becomes violent because he is *deprived* of a father. As a child, he was abandoned by his father and raised by his mother, whom he worshipped—so much that at age eleven he killed a man for having insulted her. Now alone, defenseless, a "lost little boy," he is be-friended by the kindly Tunstall (Colin Keith-Johnston), whom he comes to admire. When Tunstall is killed, Billy can respond only with wordless anguish. This is one of Newman's most inspired moments, as he progresses from a tortured expression—his head spiralling toward the ground in pain—to thoughtful tranquility, and finally to vengeful anger. Without considering morality or the consequences, he decides that he must become the law and kill the four men responsible—repeating his child-hood revenge—and thus he turns into a notorious outlaw. Later he is helped by an elderly Mexican and his young wife (Lita Milan), and Billy seduces her (the Oedipal desire fulfilled). When the man finds out, Billy feels he has nothing left, and allows Pat Garrett (John Dehner) to kill him. He has violated the sanctity of the family.

Freudian symbolism notwith-standing, the film is only occasion-ally pretentious and self-conscious; more often it is exciting, vibrant, even exuberant. Billy's instinctive sense, released in violence, also finds an outlet in eruptions of ado-lescent joy. One scene is worth citing, because it represents a rare instance of improvisation in New-man's work. Shortly after Tun-stall's death, Billy learns the names of the men he will go after, and his intense mourning turns to boister-ous jubilation: he marches around with a broom, singing, laughing, joking (Penn calls it "ecstatic grief").

The film, shot for Warners on a shoestring budget and schedule (twenty-three days), was a moder-ate commercial success, but critics were puzzled by its offbeat nature. Today it has a large following, al-though Newman says, "I still don't like the film. It's artificial." It re-mains, however, one of his best films, and it marked a major de-velopment in his acting abilities, indicating gifts for improvisation and superb physical performing. The film is also a rare instance of the perfect director-actor confluence, and it's unfortunate that Penn and Newman have never worked to-gether since.

Newman was again loaned out, for Fox's *The Long Hot Summer* (1958), the first of six films he made for director Martin Ritt and the first of seven co-starring Joanne Wood-ward. As usual, he prepared seriously—by living unrecognized for three days in Clinton, Miss., where he observed local habits and language. The film, based on two short stories and part of a novel by Faulkner, provided him with his best role to that time.

Ben Quick (Newman), a brash, opportunistic young redneck, drifts into a Mississippi town owned and run by the huge, powerful Will

THE LEFT-HANDED GUN (1958). With Alan Carney.

THE LONG HOT SUMMER (1958). With Anthony Franciosa.

THE LONG HOT SUMMER (1958). With Lee Remick.

Varner (Orson Welles), who also dominates his daughter Clara (Woodward), a 23-year-old unmarried schoolteacher. Despite Quick's reputation as a "barnburner" (arsonist), he is hired by Varner, and rapidly works his way up to a partnership in the general store and a room in the main house. Varner, like Big Daddy in *Cat on a Hot Tin Roof*, wants strong descendants, and since his son is a weakling, he decides that Clara will marry Quick, whose aggressive masculinity he admires (he calls Quick a "big stud horse"). Clara, offended by Quick's smug and vulgar manner, and by both men's treating her as property, resists.

Like Billy the Kid, Quick is an outcast, isolated from humanity because of his notorious reputation. But in temperament he's the opposite, an extreme extrovert. From the very beginning, Newman, hat down low over his forehead, eyes gleaming with ambition, projects an overwhelming confidence, self-satisfaction and, above all, electrifying virility. Cynical, arrogant, crude and unwilling to allow anything to interfere with his drive, he resembles Larry Maddux of *The Helen Morgan Story*. But now the portrayal is more than one-dimensional: behind Quick's hard blue eyes, barely hidden sneer and devilish grin there's enough intelligence, humor, charm and downright attractiveness to force our involvement in his quest for power.

This is due entirely to Newman's subtle acting, because as written the character reveals no positive traits until near the end, when he breaks down and tells Clara the truth about himself. It's a powerful scene: his voice breaking, eyes filling slowly with tears, Newman effectively depicts a man whose carefully formed cold shell is finally cracking to reveal the vulnerable soul within. The confession gives him a bond of equality with Clara that enables him to stand up decisively to Varner. But even earlier, Quick was never completely dominated by the old man. Of all the father-figures in Newman's films, Varner seems the most imposing, but Quick, unlike the weakling sons in *The Rack* and *Cat on a Hot Tin Roof*, isn't passive enough to be stepped upon.

By the time the film was being shot, in late 1957, Newman had obtained a divorce, and he and Woodward were about to be married. The genuine warmth of their relationship—their extreme ease at being together—comes through constantly, and takes much of the edge off the sexual antagonism. The characters are perfect foils: he is sexually sure, and seemingly devoid of vulnerability and humanity; she is a virgin, extremely vulnerable, and longing to express her humanity. She teaches him humility and the value of an individual; he helps her discover her sexuality.

Two scenes are among the best in their careers, partly because of the sharp dialogue by Irving Ravetch and Harriet Frank. In the first, Clara comes to see Ben in the store at night. After much childish invective and a few blunt truths, the two have pierced beneath the surface and have found the nerve endings of each other's weaknesses. Later, in the film's finest scene, Clara expresses herself more maturely, asserting that he has the wrong idea about her: she is no "trembling little rabbit, full of smoldering unsatisfied desires," but a full-grown, intelligent woman, who will not be bought and sold. She says he's too much like her father: "I gave up on him when I was nine years old, and I gave up on you the first time I ever looked into those cold blue eyes."

With his crisp, assured manner Quick sums up his honest, hard, purely sexual appraisal of life: "Well, I can see you don't like me, but you're gonna have me. It's gonna be you and me . . . Yes sir, they're gonna say, 'There goes that

THE LONG HOT SUMMER (1958). With Joanne Woodward, Anthony Franciosa, Lee Remick, Orson Welles, and Richard Anderson.

CAT ON A HOT TIN ROOF (1958). With Elizabeth Taylor.

poor old Clara Varner, whose father married her off to a dirt-scratchin', shiftless, no-good farmer who just happened by.' Well, let 'em talk. I'll tell you one thing—you're gonna wake up in the mornin' . . . smil-in'."

Newman and Woodward had much to smile about in 1958: four of his films were released, including *The Long Hot Summer,* for which he received excellent reviews and the Best Actor Award at the Cannes Film Festival (the only American honored there in '58); she won an Oscar as Best Actress for 1957's *The Three Faces of Eve;* and, before all of those events, on January 29, they were married. Their marriage has lasted over sixteen years, a rare achievement for two major stars, and they've had three daughters (Elinor, born 1959; Melissa, born 1961; Claire, born 1965). Woodward has subordinated her career to his, turning down parts if it will mean long separations, but they have also managed to make their careers coincide. Except for their two comedies, their joint screen appearances have produced excellent results; and Newman, who has called his wife "the last of the great broads," has directed her in two outstanding performances.

On January 16, two weeks before their wedding, they co-starred in a *Playhouse 90* drama, *The 80-Yard Run,* generally considered Newman's best television work. He played a college football hero who married the campus queen (Woodward). Years later, during the Depression, he is out of work, but she becomes successful on a fashion magazine. As she advances, his self-confidence dwindles. He just sits and broods, remembering his greatest moment—the 80-yard run.

Coincidentally, in the opening of his next film, *Cat on a Hot Tin Roof* (1958), Newman, as an ex-football player, is trying to relive his college athletic glories. Drinking and staggering, he attempts to jump hurdles, resulting in a painful injury that has him hobbling around on crutches during most of the film.

Newman was back at MGM, but more importantly, he was doing Tennessee Williams, and—despite the fact that Ben Gazzara had played Brick on stage—this put him in Brando country. Now he could prove decisively that he wasn't a second-rate Brando. The role was certainly another demonstration of his widening range, for Brick is in many ways the antithesis of Ben Quick. Although he too is cynical, cold and guilt-ridden, he manifests it by becoming moody, withdrawn, introverted. In addition, whereas Ben was strong and decisive, causing and participating in events, Brick is weak and passive, largely reacting to events around him. And he's anything but ambitious: while his greedy brother and sister-in-law await Big Daddy's death so they can inherit his huge fortune and plantation, and while his wife Maggie (Elizabeth Taylor) urges him to fight for his share, he merely broods and drinks. An emotionally crippled, "thirty-year-old boy," he refuses to face responsibility and truth, preferring to drown his memories in liquor.

Newman and Taylor enact striking contrasts in temperament: she is fiery, loud, animated, sensual; he is cold, quiet, immobile, dispassionate. Brick and Maggie haven't been sleeping together, and she wants him desperately, but he keeps rejecting her advances. As she talks, he replies with sarcasm, contempt and mostly indifference, speaking in a dreamy, monotonous manner, as if only half-there. In conversations with her, as with Big Daddy (Burl Ives), he stares into space, or walks away (usually toward the liquor supply), turning his back on the other party and forcing the dialogue to take place on separate planes. All of this places him in a private world, where he hides his torment and anxiety beneath a mask of detachment.

If Newman is best at enacting

CAT ON A HOT TIN ROOF (1958). With Elizabeth Taylor.

CAT ON A HOT TIN ROOF (1958). With Burl Ives.

Brick's unspoken thoughts and emotions, he's also effective in the more spirited moments, as when he screams at Maggie or Big Daddy, to prevent them from getting at the truth he wants kept buried. But exactly what the "truth" is remains unclear. In the play, Brick's fear of admitting a homosexual attachment led indirectly to his friend's death and explained his overall moodiness and passivity. But because of Hollywood's moral code, director-scriptwriter Richard Brooks had to eliminate this, and the character's motivations are considerably weakened. His hostility toward Maggie—understandable in the play—is especially confusing because it results from events that are unconvincingly outlined.

With the homosexuality expurgated, Brick's dependence upon his friend is now explained by the failure of Big Daddy to provide strength and love, and this changed emphasis does make for exciting drama. The film's key scene—not in the play—is one in which Brick confronts his father with this painful truth. As they sit in a cellar cluttered with the old man's useless antiques, he tells Big Daddy that love cannot be bought. Newman moves powerfully from anguished looks to an outburst of emotion, smashing everything in sight, finally breaking down and crying: "All I wanted was a father, not a boss . . . I wanted you

to love me." Both are in pain—Big Daddy because of cancer, Brick because his crutch has (symbolically) been broken, and they need each other's help to get upstairs. Thus the film ultimately becomes another statement of father-son alienation, and their coming to terms with it, as in *The Rack* and *Somebody Up There Likes Me*, leads the characters to a new strength (and an upbeat ending not in the play).

Despite its compromises, the film was still daring by 1958 standards, and was an enormous commercial success. It received six Oscar nominations, including one for Newman as Best Actor—his first. By now he had really arrived. The critics admired him, the public knew his name, and he no longer had to worry about Brando. He had developed, especially in his last three films, a really impressive acting ability, and a distinctive screen image.

For his final 1958 release, *Rally 'Round the Flag, Boys!*, he was again teamed with Woodward at Fox. This was his first comedy, and he was in the expert hands of Leo McCarey, who had directed Laurel and Hardy, W.C. Fields and the Marx Brothers. The Newmans are hardly in that class, and *Rally* is one of McCarey's lesser efforts, but it's often a refreshing reminder of thirties screwball farce (of which his *The*

Awful Truth was one of the best) as well as a frequently incisive satire on suburban life.

Newman is a typical harried commuter, whose wife (Woodward) spends all her time in community affairs, leaving him frustrated, and whose two sons are so hypnotized by television they hardly notice him—so he escapes with alcohol (again!) and daydreams. When the Army schedules a secret base for their town, the couple are on opposing sides: she heads the protest committee; he, a reserve officer, is "drafted" as public relations man to win over the town. Their marriage really goes downhill when she catches him in a compromising (but innocent) situation with a sexy neighbor (Joan Collins). But after many screwball happenings, they are reunited in a Keystone Kops finale involving a rocket launching and a frisky chimpanzee.

Newman is often charming, but generally, in a role Jack Lemmon would have walked through, he overacts outrageously, trying so hard to be funny we don't laugh.

RALLY 'ROUND THE FLAG, BOYS! (1958). With Joanne Woodward.

RALLY 'ROUND THE FLAG, BOYS! (1958). With Joanne Woodward.

Admittedly, some of the gags and slapstick situations are forced, as when the drunken Newman and Collins dance the cha-cha, swing on chandeliers, and fall down stairs; or when Newman is caught literally with his pants down, warding off the predatory Collins and trying to explain to the outraged Woodward. But even Rock Hudson and Doris Day would have made something of these scenes. The Newmans are reduced to mugging, exaggerated gestures and extreme over-reactions.

The Newmans were still young, but they played such older-generation types that a teenaged couple (Dwayne Hickman and Tuesday Weld) were added for the younger audience. Incredibly, Hickman, who does an inventive caricature of an American teenager, plays it as Marlon Brando! Decked out in Brando's *Wild One* outfit, he mumbles, stutters, and ambles about with the familiar anguished look. Newman, who had played an adolescent just three films earlier, was now being supplanted as a Brandoesque rebel.

50

Newman has often expressed a fascination with men who possess assets that impress people in this country: external attractiveness, ingratiating charm, wealth, virility—men who can easily seduce women and who feel equally at home drinking with the guys. He believes that these glamorous heroes must be shown to have the "seed of corruption" in them, so that we will learn something about the men we admire. When they succeed, they lose their souls, and either they must recognize this, and cleanse themselves, or, if they fail to do so, we must recognize it, and condemn them. Larry Maddux and Ben Quick were such characters, and others keep appearing in Newman's films. The process by which the seed is planted, and nourished until it grows into a noxious weed, is a major theme in his 1959-1963 period.

In Warners' *The Young Philadelphians* (1959), for example, he plays a young lawyer who abandons all values in search of success. Directed by Vincent Sherman, who had made some of Joan Crawford's tough career-woman vehicles, this slick soap opera actually finds Newman in a Crawford role. Tony Lawrence is born into poverty, and his mother brings him up to believe that social position, good contacts and money are all that matter. At first he resists, but events harden

THE SEED OF CORRUPTION

him into a cynical opportunist, and he sets out on an amoral journey to the top of his law firm. He double-crosses, romances and ingratiates himself to success, but loses all his youthful idealism, and becomes unhappy with himself. Finally deciding that success isn't worth the price, he chooses integrity, risking the enmity of a prominent family by defending an alcoholic friend. But the film compromises, enabling Tony to win the case *and* marry the rich girl and stay in high society.

Tony, the ruthless opportunist, is superficially another Ben Quick, but here the writing is perfunctory and Newman responds with an appropriately routine portrayal. He goes through the motions well, conveying the smiling, eager innocent at the beginning, and the intense, jaded conniver later on. But it's all on the surface, with no depth of feeling. Tony doesn't even have the underlying devilish charm, only an attractive face. And at crucial moments—when Tony's girl marries another man and when he finds out who his real father is—Newman falls back on heavy breathing, rapid blinking and feverish lip movements.

THE YOUNG PHILADELPHIANS (1959). With Barbara Rush.

He and the film were panned, and *Variety* commented that he "plays his role as though he had contractual obligations to fulfill and found them distasteful." That was exactly right: Newman, who had been unhappy with Warners since 1954, was anxious to get out. In August, 1959—three months after *The Young Philadelphians* opened—he bought out his contract, which had three years yet to run, for $500,000. It was worth the price: Newman had earned as little as $25,000 a picture at Warners, which would gladly loan him out at $75,000 and pocket the difference. Now, as a free agent, he would ask—and get—$200,000 a film.

Before this, Newman had already demonstrated independence by leaving Hollywood a second time and returning to Broadway. After completing *The Young Philadelphians,* he accepted the lead opposite Geraldine Page in Tennessee Williams' *Sweet Bird of Youth.* At last he had a Williams role that was his alone, and when he did the movie version he would be in no one's shadow. The play, directed by Elia Kazan, opened on March 10, 1959, and was a huge success. Chance Wayne, the attractive, aging adolescent who longs for fame in Hollywood and ruthlessly pursues any means to get it, is the quintessential Newman character,

THE YOUNG PHILADELPHIANS (1959). With Robert Vaughn.

and the actor was magnificent, getting the best reviews of his career up to that point.

Newman returned to the stage because he believed that he had become too complacent in Hollywood; he wanted to place himself on trial before a live audience: "There's always that terrible fear, that one day your fraud will be discovered and you'll be back in the dog kennel business. That's why it's good to work on Broadway as well as Hollywood. You know you'll get the hell kicked out of you here once in a while—but if you don't you'll fall back on a lot of successful mannerisms." This self-improvement also included continued studies with Lee Strasberg at the Actors

SWEET BIRD OF YOUTH (1959). With Geraldine Page and Sidney Blackmer.

FROM THE TERRACE (1960). With Joanne Woodward.

Studio, as well as voice lessons to eliminate what Newman felt was an annoying hoarseness.

On April 7, the Newmans' first child, Elinor Theresa, was born; as "Nell Potts," she would give superb performances in two Newman-directed films. Toward the end of his run in *Sweet Bird of Youth*, Newman began shooting *From the Terrace* with Woodward during the day. In January, 1960 he left the

play and returned to Hollywood to complete the film. He had appeared for 42 weeks, missing none of the 336 performances.

From the Terrace (1960) was an odd choice for the liberated actor to make, since it was basically the kind of film he had hated to do at Warners. Although based on a John O'Hara novel, it's another *Young Philadelphians:* a slick, soggy soap opera, set from the late forties to the late fifties, with Newman as an angry young opportunist from Philadelphia. Again the moral (which undoubtedly attracted him) is that the drive for wealth and power corrupts innocence and love. Here there's more of a motivation, the old reliable one: his father hates him. He tells his cold, nasty father (Leon Ames), "All I ever wanted was to be friends with you," then defiantly rejects the family's fairly substantial steel mill. He wants more—to make $5 million by age forty, to be better than his old man.

On his way up the cynical path to Wall Street, he ignores his marriage, driving his once-sweet wife (Woodward) to bitchery and into the bed of an old flame. He works intensively to become a high financier, but suddenly realizes how empty his life is; unlike Tony Lawrence, he drops out completely, leaving his failed marriage and flourishing career to marry a wholesome small-town woman.

Newman battles valiantly with incredible soap opera contrivances, crises and turgid dialogue, but he loses. He's worst in his scenes with the decent young woman (Ina Balin), because the relationship is improbable, their talk about love is ponderous, and he's not convincing as the shy, gentle lover. (We've seen him earlier as sexually confident and aggressive, and besides, Newman is not very good at ex-pressing tenderness.) He's excellent at the beginning, indicating bitterness toward his father with contemptuous facial expressions, although here, as elsewhere, his tendency to show tension or self-absorption by blinking and looking away during conversations is overdone.

But with Woodward, he and the film really come to life. During their first meetings, as he comes on strong and she resists, the antagonism, tinged with overtones of desperate sexuality, reminds us of *The Long Hot Summer*. Then, in their marriage, the roles are reversed: he becomes immersed in business, and she becomes sexually frustrated, creating a highly-charged tension between them. There's a beautifully acted scene near the end when, like Maggie the Cat, she pathetically flaunts her sexuality at him and he merely sits there with a world-weary look. Ironically, Woodward (and to an extent the script) make the wife so vital and pathetic that it's hard to accept her as a bitch, and the ending—in which we are supposed to find cathartic release in his leaving her—makes little sense.

Nonetheless, this film, like all the others after *The Long Hot Summer*, was a substantial commercial success. By now, Newman was such a big box-office draw that he landed the coveted star-

FROM THE TERRACE (1960). As Alfred Eaton.

ring role of Ari Ben Canaan, the Palestinian underground leader, in Otto Preminger's *Exodus* (1960). After completing *From the Terrace*, the Newmans left for Israel, where he spent several weeks before shooting, getting the feel of the country and its people.

Exodus is an ambitious, 3½-hour adaptation of Leon Uris' best-selling novel about the founding of Israel in 1947. It centers on the successful escape, masterminded by Ari, of over 600 Jewish refugees from Cyprus to Palestine; the underground activities in Palestine; and the first Israeli-Arab conflicts following partition. Surrounding these and other events are many personal dramas, including Ari's

EXODUS (1960). With Eva Marie Saint and John Derek.

EXODUS (1960). With Eva Marie Saint.

romance with American nurse Kitty Fremont (Eva Marie Saint) and his friendship with a sympathetic Arab chieftain (John Derek). It's a stirring and visually beautiful film, but it contains one of Newman's least exciting performances.

Some contend that Newman's motivational Method conflicted with Preminger's authoritarian approach; others that he was miscast. But Ari is the kind of dedicated, single-minded loner Newman is expert at—except, of course, that the dedication is to a cause, not to himself. When he insults the well-meaning Cypriot, Mandria, his friends rebuke him, saying Mandria is a real friend, and he replies: "When the showdown comes, we will always stand alone. Mandria will sell us out like all the others. We have no friends, except ourselves." Those lines are also in the novel, but they could almost have been written expressly for Newman, whose self-sufficient characters often speak in this manner.

The real problem is that New-man never gives Ari warmth or hu-manity. His initial impatience, hos-tility, arrogance and indifference to individual problems are under-standable, since he is planning cru-cial events. But even when he is supposed to be getting warmer, more understanding, aware that outsiders *can* be trusted (Kitty, a Christian, becomes deeply commit-ted to the cause), his demeanor re-mains almost exactly the same. He never comes to life until the last scene, a passionate funeral oration, and by then it's too late. There's none of the charm or vitality that makes us interested in even the

most vicious of Newman's anti-heroes. In the one instance where Newman is supposed to be funny—his impersonation of a British officer—he is forced and un-easy.

Exodus grossed more than any previous Newman film (and only *Butch Cassidy* has surpassed it), but with all his box-office success, he still needed a part that would reconfirm his stature as a film actor. In 1961 he got one in *The Hustler*. Fast Eddie Felson was his best role ever, and Newman re-sponded to the occasion with his most creative performance.

Director-scriptwriter Robert

Rossen provides a realistic glimpse into the grimy world of the pool hall, and makes it a battleground on which strength and courage are tested. Fast Eddie is not the traditional, heroic white knight. He's a crafty pool hustler, a man who makes his money by tricking opponents into thinking he's not as good as he really is. But he wants more than cheap hustling—his ambition is to beat the country's top player, Minnesota Fats, and this places him with Newman's other obsessed seekers of grand goals.

Newman really gets inside the character—makes us feel his desperate drive. In the opening scenes, depicting Eddie's marathon match with Fats (Jackie Gleason), he personifies overwhelming confidence, coolness and conceit; as Eddie puts it, he's "fast and loose." He grins, moves with assurance around the table, and baits Fats: "I dreamed about this game, fat man . . . This is my table now. I own it." But there's an underlying insecurity, and a self-destructive tendency. He doesn't know when to stop, and even though he's $18,000 ahead, he won't quit until Fats is demolished. His cockiness leads him to become sloppy and eventually to fall into a drunken stupor. Fats, in contrast, remains casual and unruffled, and he takes all of Eddie's money. As Fats' manager, the crafty, snakelike Gordon (George C. Scott), says, Eddie's "a loser."

Eddie's arrogance is unpleasant and his lack of restraint is pathetic, but he's partially redeemed by his affair with Sarah (Piper Laurie), a self-pitying, lame, worn-out alcoholic, whose vulnerability attracts him. It's a splendidly enacted relationship between two derelicts, beginning as a casual pickup and developing into tentative affection. Initially all they do is drink and make love, and, even though Sarah realizes he is not much better than a bum, she (like many women in Newman films) wants more. The turning point occurs when Eddie again loses his restraint and shows off to some men he's hustling, whereupon they break his thumbs. Now, for the first time, he needs Sarah's help, and their relationship deepens as he realizes his dependence upon *her*.

And she's the only person he can talk to about what most moves him. In a picnic on a hillside—one of the best scenes in Newman's career —Eddie explains that he lost his restraint with the small-time players because he had to show them what pool is like "when it's really great." He says that at times he becomes so immersed in pool that his arm and the cue perform as one beautifully functioning organism. This speech is rendered almost poetic by Newman's passionate expression and delivery; together with earlier scenes in which we saw Eddie's movements in the game and his look

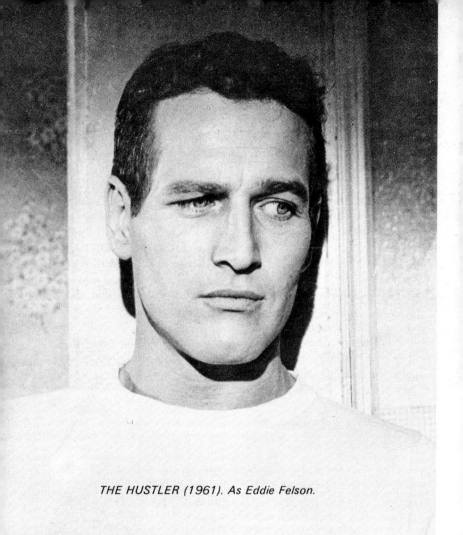

THE HUSTLER (1961). As Eddie Felson.

THE HUSTLER (1961). With George C. Scott (at his left).

of admiration at Fats' grace, it convinces us that whether he wins or loses, Eddie is alive only when playing pool.

Sarah is moved to express her love, but the closest he can come is: "You need the words?" She does, but he can't say them. And ultimately, whatever love he may feel is overshadowed by the all-consuming need to get back at Fats. He cruelly rejects his fatherly manager (Myron McCormick), who has no such lofty ambitions, and becomes a slave to Gordon, who says he'll always be a loser unless he rids himself of Sarah.

Eddie rejects her in order to win a billiards match, and she commits suicide. This situation is uncomfortably contrived, but Newman is affecting in the scene where Eddie sees her body and realizes what he's done. He kneels, holds out his hand helplessly, and rolls his head around in wordless pain—just as Billy the Kid did at Tunstall's death.

Once again the "seed of corruption" has almost destroyed a man's soul. Here it is a drive to win at all costs, not a lust for wealth, but the result is the same. When Eddie returns to battle Fats, his humor, jauntiness, confidence and feeling for the game are gone; he is solemn, mean, out for revenge. He beats Fats quickly, and stands up to Gordon, saying that otherwise her death will have meant nothing. In one of Newman's most forceful moments of anguish, he says: "We really stuck the knife in her . . . I loved her. I traded her in on a pool game." He has said the words, and although it's too late for her, it's something of a personal victory. Eddie may be almost completely broken, but he has gained some humanity.

This is Newman's most balanced characterization—on the one hand, ruthless ambition, arrogant confidence and inability to express love; on the other, vulnerability, recognition of dependence and genuine self-realization—and he brings it all off to perfection. It was his most critically acclaimed performance to that time. The film received nine Oscar nominations, including Newman's second as Best Actor. The award went to the vastly inferior Maximilian Schell (*Judgment at Nuremberg*), but Newman did win the British Academy Award.

After this high point, anything would be a let-down, but *Paris Blues*, released about a month later, was especially lightweight. In this, his second film for Martin Ritt and his fourth with Joanne Woodward, Newman is an American jazz trombonist living in Paris, devoting himself to writing a concerto. He has an affair with an American tourist (Woodward), who wants him to return with her to the U.S., but he believes that marriage would interfere with his career, and decides to remain. The thin plot is dressed up with Duke Ellington jazz, Louis Armstrong in a jam session, French New Wave-influenced shots of the lovers wandering around Paris, and a subsidiary romance involving Sidney Poitier and Diahann Carroll.

As in *The Hustler*, Newman plays a man whose devotion to making his talent better than second-rate precludes love. But he was natural as the pool player, and convinced us—through his movements, dialogue and expressions—of his feelings for the game, whereas he is unconvincing as the musician. There are many shots of him playing (Newman actually learned the trombone for the part, although someone else dubbed the music), with Newman superficially demonstrating involvement through typically intense facial expressions. But compare Eddie's almost mystical speech about pool with these perfunctory, mechanically recited lines: "Honey, I *live* music—morning, noon, the whole night. Everything else is just icing on the cake, you dig?"

Newman and Woodward are again so natural together that the

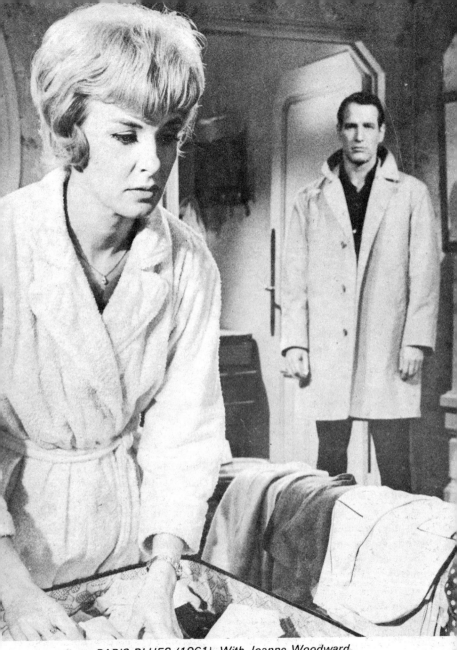

PARIS BLUES (1961). With Joanne Woodward.

PARIS BLUES (1961). With Diahann Carroll, Sidney Poitier, and Joanne Woodward.

film does become interesting in a few of their scenes. Untypically, she is immediately the more aggressive of the two; moved by his music, she displays genuine emotion, but he is so defensive and self-centered that he becomes hostile, awkward, obnoxious. Later, the relationship settles into the usual Newman-Woodward mold: she is determined to make something more of it, and he remains detached—willing to show slight af-

fection but incapable of being sincerely tender. In their final bedroom scene, the two superbly perform a progression from spontaneous domestic affection, to growing alienation, to his indifferent rejection of her love.

In 1962, Newman recreated two of his roles from other media. The first was Chance Wayne in Williams' *Sweet Bird of Youth*. He had carefully studied the character during his ten-month Broadway run,

SWEET BIRD OF YOUTH (1962). With Shirley Knight.

SWEET BIRD OF YOUTH (1962). With Geraldine Page.

and it's one of his most deeply felt and affecting screen portrayals. Again he's the attractive young man ruthlessly pursuing the American Dream of success, coldly exploiting people and rejecting the love that might save him. Chance has only one talent—sexual prowess—and he's been bumming around for several years, satisfying rich women in the hope that he can find fame in Hollywood. He picks up a faded film star, Alexandra Del Lago (magnificently played by Geraldine Page), who is hooked on vodka, hashish, oxygen and young studs. She promises to get him a screen test, and they drive to his Southern hometown, where he plans to find his sweetheart, Heavenly (Shirley Knight), and take her along to Hollywood. He doesn't know that on his last visit he left her pregnant, that she had an abortion, and that her father, the powerful Boss Finley (Ed Begley), is out to get him.

Newman is impeccable as the smiling, confident phony who acts like a celebrity—dropping names, giving large tips, arrogantly stating: "Just because a man's successful doesn't mean he has to forget his hometown." He's also frighteningly sneaky and conniving, as he charms Alexandra while recording what she's saying for blackmail purposes. But he's ultimately pathetic: a desperately insecure man, addicted to amphetamines, obsequi- ously attending to Alexandra and performing as a lover at her whim. His mask of swaggering bravura really disappears when he tries to see Heavenly. He becomes confused and desperate—pacing, rubbing his hands together, pleading urgently over the phone.

Flashbacks (not in the play) show him as a younger man—smiling, innocent, eager to marry Heavenly, but persuaded by Finley (who scorns Chance's poor background) to leave town and pursue success. Thus Chance was corrupted, and began to use his sexuality to get ahead.

Chance doesn't make it, but he keeps dreaming. On his previous visit, he tells Heavenly that he's learned how to "beat the game." Newman has never been more convincing as an intense man on the make. With a ruthless look, he says he will return a success next time: "I got the key, baby—I got the know- how . . . for me there's one quick way." She wants him as he is, but he can't stop: "All my life I've been on the outside, and time is running out . . . they got places for the old and the sick and the homeless, but there is no place at all for the failures." He rejects her to become a beach boy: "Don't ask me to give up my dream."

Now it's too late, and in another effective scene, Heavenly refuses to come with him, ignoring his

SWEET BIRD OF YOUTH (1962). With Rip Torn, Jim Douglas, and Corey Allen.

agonized pleas, and leaving him stunned, anguished, alone with his dream. Later, Alexandra gets a call from Walter Winchell, informing her that she's not a has-been after all. Chance stands nervously in the background, cracking his knuckles, biting his fingers, leaning forward, reminding her to mention him. She hangs up without saying a word about Chance, then tells him: "You have gone past something you couldn't afford to go past: your time, your youth. You've passed it—it's all you had and you passed it." She says he can be her lover until she tires of him, but there will be no screen test. Finally realizing the truth about himself, Chance decides to remain behind and face what Boss Finley has in store.

Newman says that Chance must take his beating to expiate his sins: "He's saying to you—all of you—'look at me and recognize whatever there is of me in you'." Like Fast Eddie, he must be punished for his arrogance. In the play, which ends with his being castrated by Finley's son, the expiation is clear, but the film's ending makes no sense. First, the castration is changed to a quick blow across the face with a stick, which, rather unconvincingly, causes total disfigurement. But even that can gener-

HEMINGWAY'S ADVENTURES OF A YOUNG MAN (1962). As the Battler.

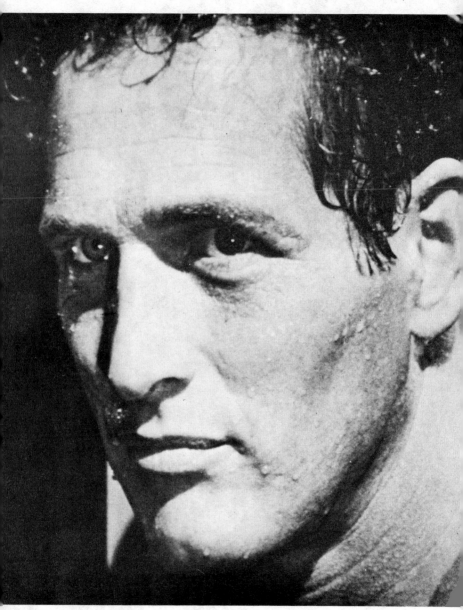

HUD (1963). As Hud Bannon.

ously be construed as "taking away lover boy's meal ticket." What's really ludicrous is that Heavenly shows up and leaves with Chance. Despite the film's many contrivances and excesses, it has worked as a story of a man's pathetic downfall, but his getting the girl after all is absurd. The culprit, as in *Cat on a Hot Tin Roof*, is director-writer Richard Brooks, although perhaps the real blame belongs to Hollywood, the Kingdom of Compromise.

That same year Newman recreated his television role, "The Battler," for a cameo appearance in *Hemingway's Adventures of a Young Man.* He ignored Hollywood tradition that a big star should not do bit parts, because he liked the role, and wanted to compare his two performances to see how much he'd learned about acting since 1955. He also enjoyed working with Martin Ritt. Finally, Newman had been playing many roles—of which Chance was the epitome—that emphasized his good looks, and he welcomed a character part, one that would make him truly ugly, so that audiences could stop being distracted by his face and start paying attention to his performance. The irony is that when Newman comes on with his scarred, misshapen face, one is distracted by the skillful makeup ("Is that *really* Paul Newman?") and pays little attention to

the performance anyway.

The film, based on Hemingway's autobiographical "Nick Adams" stories, depicts the picaresque experiences of an aspiring writer (Richard Beymer) who leaves his home in 1917 to learn about life. Near the beginning, the young man, thrown off a freight train, encounters the punch drunk fighter and his black manager and friend, Bugs (Juano Hernandez). The Battler, in his fifties, was once a top fighter, but he declined into second-rate matches, prison and panhandling (Rocky Graziano in reverse!). As he and Nick sit in the woods by a fire, the pitiful, half-alive Battler speaks hoarsely, sometimes mumbling incoherently, about his life. He gropes pathetically for his thoughts and memories, makes useless swinging gestures in the air, and reflexively punches his fist into his palm—a man barely in control of his mind or muscles.

This is the kind of self-effacing, grotesque-makeup part critics often like, and many thought he brought compassion as well as physical reality to it. Others believed that he overplayed it almost to the point of caricature; Bosley Crowther of *The New York Times* said, "It is Paul Newman's very good fortune that he isn't recognizable . . . for he is simply terrible."

Newman is recognizable and simply superb in his next film, *Hud*

HUD (1963). With Brandon de Wilde.

(1963). The title character, a cattleman in contemporary Texas, is the quintessence of Newman's amoral, opportunistic loners: he's arrogant, seething with ambition, incapable of much warmth or affection. He brawls, drinks heavily, takes women with crude assurance ("The only question I ever ask any woman is 'What time is your husband coming home?' "), and doesn't give a damn about anyone except himself. Newman brings his familiar characteristics to perfection: the cynical, aloof manner; the nasty, contemptuous voice; the sly, insinuating smile. He's a model of casual defiance and detachment, as he roars through the dusty town in his pink Cadillac; lounges broodingly on a fence, swigging a pint of bourbon; stands insolently, hands on hips, hat down low over his forehead.

Hud resembles Ben Quick, which isn't surprising, since director Martin Ritt and writers Ravetch and Frank also did *The Long Hot Summer*. Like Quick, he is considerably sexy and charming, which attracts women and drinking buddies. He's the best example of Newman's idea of the glamorous, captivating, virile, but essentially rotten men we mistakenly admire; according to Newman, the film is meant to expose his underlying corruption. The drama revolves around the discovery of Hud's amorality by Lon (Brandon de Wilde), his seventeen-year-old nephew. Lon admires his uncle, but is ultimately torn between Hud's hedonism and the high moral principles of Hud's father, aging Homer Bannon (Melvyn Douglas).

When Homer's cattle become diseased, Hud wants to sell them quickly, but Homer refuses to spread an epidemic, and has them destroyed. Hud really becomes despicable as he tries to have his father certified incompetent, so that he can take over the ranch. Like Chance Wayne, he's afraid of ending up in poverty: "You don't look out for yourself, the only helping hand you'll ever get is when they lower the box." When Hud tries to rape Alma (Patricia Neal), the housekeeper Lon admires, the boy finally turns against him; after Homer dies, he quits the ranch, leaving Hud by himself.

Whereas Quick turned out to be a good guy after all, and Fast Eddie and Chance matured through pain and punishment, Hud is untouched and unregenerate to the very end. Refusing to accept his guilt, he says he's only as corrupt as everyone else; as Lon leaves, Hud yells, "The world's so full of crap a man's going to get into it sooner or later, whether he's careful or not." Then he goes into the house, grabs a beer, drinks, leans on the door and looks in Lon's direction. Instead of showing remorse, he sneers cynically,

HUD (1963). With Melvyn Douglas.

dismisses Lon with a contemptuous wave, and goes inside, closing the door decisively. He may not be entirely pleased with himself, and he may need the solace of drink, but he's tough enough to shut out the world and remain utterly alone.

Newman says the studio wanted Hud to reform, but the filmmakers refused. The spirit of "no compromise" supposedly guided them throughout, and Newman was disappointed that, despite the intention to portray a complete heel, many people considered Hud a hero. But this is natural, since the film is actually filled with compromises. For instance, Homer, the representative of goodness, is self-righteous, inflexible, full of solemn, pious platitudes, and generally unappealing, while Hud is vital, life-affirming and humorous. Furthermore, Homer's contempt for Hud, which he justifies by Hud's having never given a damn, seems unfair. Apparently he soured on Hud when the latter was in his teens, and thus the boy was denied love when he most needed it. This again brings up the father-son alienation theme, and it makes us sympathetic toward Hud.

Even in his relations with others, Hud is not entirely despicable. He displays some tenderness toward Lon, especially in the scene in which they get drunk together. There's a touching moment as Hud

says, somewhat sadly, "Get all the good you can out of seventeen, 'cause it sure wears out in one hell of a hurry." In his cynical conversations with Alma, he has Quick's insolent sexual confidence, but Alma is experienced, earthy and just as cynical, and she even seems to encourage his sly innuendos, making it a match of equals rather than a one-sided sexual pursuit.

Finally, how does an actor play a man whose overpowering charm attracts people, without attracting the audience as well? Of course this is a problem inherent in all of Newman's sexy villains, but at least with Quick and Eddie the charming traits prepare us for their reformations, while with Hud they work against the concept of his worthlessness. At this stage in his career, Newman was so appealing that it was hard to consider him as completely rotten.

Hud received a greater number of favorable reviews than any other Newman film, did well commercially, and was nominated for seven Oscars. Awards went to Neal, Douglas and cinematographer James Wong Howe. Newman, up for his third Oscar, said, "I'd like to see Sidney Poitier get it. I'd be proud to win it for a role I really had to reach for." He got his wish: Poitier *(Lilies of the Field)* won. In any case, *Hud* found Newman near the top of his form, and it was a

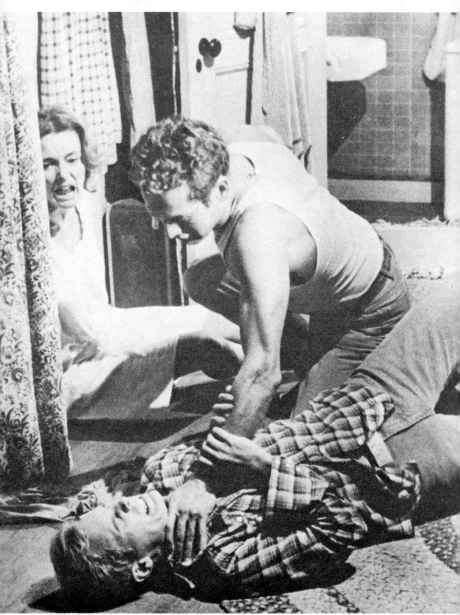

HUD (1963). With Patricia Neal and Brandon de Wilde.

culmination of the "seed of corruption" theme. To be sure, subsequent characters would be corrupt, and would coldly reject the world, but never as a result of such intense ambition.

And for Newman the movie star, *Hud* was a major event. The ads stated: "Paul Newman *is* Hud." It was one of the few times this kind of advertising had been done, and it attested to his importance: audiences were not going to see a character named Hud, but an actor named Newman. With everyone talking about the decline of Hollywood stars, it was a bold affirmation that strong personalities would still attract audiences.

Freedom involves responsibility. When a star like Newman, given the opportunity to choose roles freely and determine his own image, makes so many poor choices, his judgment must be held accountable. After *Hud*, he scraped the bottom with three "light" films in a row. Previously he had made only one comedy, and perhaps he wanted to prove that he could be funny (he also did an off-Broadway comedy in 1964), but his selection of scripts that nobody could rescue showed little courage; in fact it provided a built-in excuse ("Of course the material is so terrible it's hardly Newman's fault . . . ").

A New Kind of Love (1963), a tasteless sex farce that must have looked bad even in script form, is Newman's worst film. It's a rehash of the old Hollywood cliche: a plain, mannish woman foolishly devotes herself to a career instead of doing what women are supposed to do —hunt for husbands. But give her beauty treatments, a new hairdo and expensive clothes and she'll straighten out and find a man. The new twist is that after her metamorphosis, the man mistakes her for a prostitute. Although she's humiliated, she encourages his misconception, telling him lurid stories about herself until—lo and behold—he falls in love with her! The implication: if fulfilling a man's infantile sex fantasies is the only way

COOL HAND NEWMAN

to get him, it's better than being an ordinary career woman.

Joanne Woodward plays the masculine woman, a fashion designer who, with blonde wig and garish makeup, actually looks more hideous than before, and Newman plays a sportswriter whose "athletics" with blondes has kept him from winning the Pulitzer Prize. He's in the customary role of alcoholic satyr, but now we're supposed to find that hilarious. As usual, he has some effective lecherous leers and self-disgusted expressions, but as in his first comedy, he's generally stiff and heavy-handed.

The setting is a gaudy Paris, and director Melville Shavelson brings in everything but the bidet to dress up this belabored men's room joke—haute couture fashion, Maurice Chevalier in a guest spot, sight gags galore, endless camera tricks, and fantasy scenes that equate sex with athletic events like bicycle races and football matches—but nothing can hide the underlying rottenness. No wonder the Newmans did not again appear together on screen until 1969.

After this nadir the only way to go was up, but Newman did not exactly scale the heights in *The Prize* (1964).

He had wanted to grow a beard, but MGM refused: "I put up one hell of a fight. But it's their $4 million so I guess they had the right! Those poor idiots! They kept saying things like 'Gable's worst flop was *Parnell*, and that was the only movie he wore a beard in'." But Newman did enjoy making *The Prize*, and it's rather entertaining, though silly. Director Mark Robson and scriptwriter Ernest Lehman (both of *From the Terrace*) transformed the relatively serious Irving Wallace novel into a glossy blend of comedy, suspense, melodrama, romance, sex and international intrigue.

The complicated story concerns a group of Nobel Prize winners gathered in Stockholm for the ceremonies. Newman is the winner in Literature, although he's written only cheap detective thrillers (under pseudonyms) for the past five years. Another hard-drinking womanizer, he has plenty of booze, and a beautiful Swedish official (Elke Sommer) assigned to him. But he's distracted from these long enough to suspect that the Physics prizewinner (Edward G. Robinson) has been kidnapped by the Communists and replaced by a double. Naturally, nobody believes him,

A NEW KIND OF LOVE (1963). With Robert Clary.

but he persists in investigating and becomes involved in wild adventures. In the end he rescues the scientist and wins the woman.

It's basically ersatz Hitchcock, with ingredients from *Foreign Correspondent* and especially *North by Northwest* (also scripted by Lehman). But the Newman character is insubstantial, the relationships are superficial, there are too many distracting subplots, and the mood shifts too abruptly from ultra-serious to tongue-in-cheek. Still, Cary Grant might have risen above the material, whereas Newman sinks. Although he delivers some amusing lines with obvious delight, and is fitfully charming (and always virile), his comedy is as self-conscious as ever. Consider the much-publicized scene in which Newman, chased by thugs, winds up at a nudists' meeting. He wraps himself in a towel, and, wanting the police to come, deliberately causes a commotion (a situation lifted from *North by Northwest*, where it was an auction). Where Grant might be subtle and spontaneously light-hearted, Newman is heavy-handed and stiff.

Newman finally got to wear a beard and moustache in *What a*

A NEW KIND OF LOVE (1963). With Joanne Woodward.

THE PRIZE (1964). At the nudists' meeting.

Way to Go! (1964), probably because they fit Hollywood's idea of what an eccentric painter looks like. Written by Betty Comden and Adolph Green and directed by J. Lee Thompson, this superproduction had a $5 million budget, elaborate sets, and Shirley MacLaine with six leading men, 72 gowns and 72 hairstyles—all for the purpose of stating that money is the root of all evil! Like *A New Kind of Love*, it's a pathetic pastiche of sex comedy, satire, fantasy and pretentious techniques, which support a one-joke story: a woman wants to live a simple life, but has the "misfortune" to marry men who become millionaires, and who die shortly

thereafter, leaving her hopelessly wealthy.

Newman had the good fortune to appear in only a small portion of this disaster. He's the second of five husbands—a down-and-out American painter who drives a taxi in Paris and has invented a machine that converts sound into oil paintings. The couple are poor and happy until MacLaine feeds classical music into the machine, resulting in a successful painting. Newman becomes rich, builds more and more machines, and gets so involved in his work (another obsessed artist!) he ignores his wife. Eventually his machines rebel, and strangle him. As if the inane plot and trite parody

THE PRIZE (1964). With Elke Sommer and Edward G. Robinson.

of modern art were not enough,
Newman is upstaged by a
painter-chimpanzee (as he is by a
bear in *Judge Roy Bean*). No actor
could triumph in this, although
Newman is surprisingly amusing
when he talks about art in almost a
Graziano voice, and when he "conducts" his machines into a frenzy.

The Outrage (1964), in which
Newman played a villainous,
lecherous Mexican bandit and killer, was a much-needed change of
pace, and he regarded it as a real
challenge: "He was an absolute

primitive, which I had never
played, with an entirely different
sense of movement and . . . an accent I was not familiar with . . . I
did it because I didn't think I could
do it."* To prepare, he spent two
weeks in Mexico, studying accents
and voice qualities. Determined to
depart radically from previous
roles, he wore a false nose, dark
contact lenses, scraggly black hair, a
moustache and a scruffy beard. Like
the Battler, Juan Carrasco was a

* Robin Bean, "Success Begins at Forty," p.
7.

character part in which Newman could escape his usual appearance and voice, and he regards the performance as one of his best.

Newman's fifth film for Martin Ritt, *The Outrage* was based on the classic Japanese film *Rashomon* (1951) by Kurosawa, and an American stage version (1959). Both had been set in eighth-century Japan, but Ritt transplanted the tale to the Southwestern U.S. following the Civil War. In its original context, the ritualistic examination of the nature of truth was effective, but it seems ponderous, stilted and ludicrous as a Western. And Ritt's veering between realism and stylization, serious drama and farce, deprives us of a consistent focus. Except for impressive photography by James Wong Howe *(Hud)*, the film is a failure.

Carrasco has been convicted of raping a woman (Claire Bloom) and murdering her husband (Laurence Harvey), but four eye-witness accounts conflict. All agree that the bandit raped the woman, but only one claims that he committed the murder. Despite the message— that truth is relative—Newman plays Carrasco in almost the same way in all versions but the last. Sadistic, self-satisfied and defiant, Carrasco snarls, sneers, struts and swaggers with macho arrogance, to conceal the fact that he can only be

WHAT A WAY TO GO (1964). With Shirley MacLaine.

THE OUTRAGE (1964). With Laurence Harvey.

THE OUTRAGE (1964). With Claire Bloom and Laurence Harvey.

powerful by tying a man to a tree and raping his wife. A rough social outcast, with half-human manner and pure animal instincts, he has affinities with Rocky Graziano and Billy the Kid. But he's an extreme version—totally amoral, concerned only with pleasure and self-preservation. In the final, farcically played account, the three characters suddenly change. Carrasco becomes cowardly, grovelling, whining and willing to reform if the woman will marry him.

The role allows Newman to give a bravura performance, not unlike Toshiro Mifune's in the Kurosawa film, and the stylization would fit the story if everybody else weren't playing it so straight. As it is, the performance seems too showy, broad, exaggerated—Newman doing a stunt and relishing it. Some critics aptly noted that his accent and hoarse, growling voice made him sound like a parody of the stock Mexican villains. Perhaps the men Newman studied really spoke that way, but it comes over as fairly humorous, and by the time the comical version appears, it doesn't seem any funnier than what we've already

THE OUTRAGE (1964). As Carrasco.

BABY WANT A KISS (1964). In the stage production, with Joanne Woodward.

LADY L (1966). With Sophia Loren.

seen. Newman deserves credit for trying something boldly different, but it just doesn't work. The film was commercially unsuccessful.

After completing it, Newman returned to the stage, to co-star with Woodward in *Baby Want a Kiss.* They went into this off-Broadway comedy—their first stage work together since *Picnic*—to benefit the Actors Studio, giving up their lucrative movie salaries to make $117.50 a week each. The play, written by their friend James Costigan and directed by Frank Corsaro, opened on April 14, 1964, and was scheduled for a limited run of four months, because Newman believes long runs make an actor stale. He said he had read some 150 plays since *Sweet Bird of Youth,* and had chosen Costigan's "adult fairy tale" because it was unconventional and thought-provoking.

LADY L (1966). With Sophia Loren.

Walter Kerr of *The New York Herald Tribune* said that it was about "the kind of plastic people who are now being produced by the American cults of success, beauty, virility and socially accepted neuroses." In other words, it was another vehicle about the corruption brought about by success. Like the Newmans, the characters are a famous Hollywood couple—an "aging juvenile and a fading ingenue"—who everyone thinks are happily married. But unlike the Newmans, they are flamboyant,

and really hate each other. They visit an unsuccessful writer-friend (Costigan) and disillusion him by revealing their real natures.

Newman received some good reviews, although he was still not considered a major comedy actor. The play generally didn't overwhelm the critics, but because of the stars' box-office power, it was almost completely sold out for the entire run.

Around this time it was announced that Newman and Sophia Loren would co-star in a film of Arthur Miller's *After the Fall,* which never materialized. Instead the two were cast in *Lady L,* and in August, when his play closed, he left for Europe. *Lady L* seemed a doomed project from the start. Hollywood had wanted to film Romain Gary's novel as far back as 1958; various directors, including George Cukor, had been scheduled. Tony Curtis and Gina Lollobrigida were signed, but quit after arguments over unsatisfactory scripts. Finally, Peter Ustinov took over as writer-director, and transformed the serious film into a serio-comedy. The film was completed in the spring of 1965, but MGM thought it was such a catastrophe that its release was delayed until May, 1966, almost two months after Newman's next film had opened. It disappeared shortly thereafter; at a cost of $2 million, it is one of Newman's greatest flops.

Newman is a charming, Robin Hood-style thief and bomb-throwing anarchist in turn-of-the-century Paris. He meets Loren in a bordello, where she works as a laundress, and they fall in love. Then he joins an underground revolutionary movement in Switzerland, and plans to assassinate a prince; in the meantime Loren meets a lord (David Niven), who offers to save Newman from the police if she will marry him. She makes an arrangement whereby she can have both men—a bizarre

HARPER (1966). With Janet Leigh.

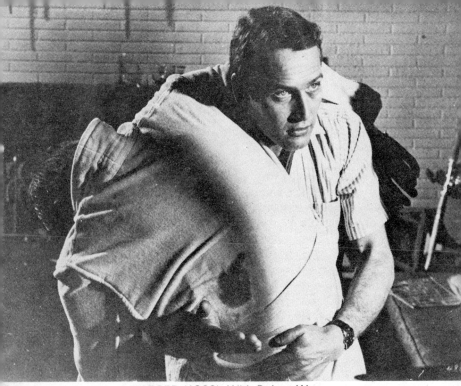

HARPER (1966). With Robert Wagner.

ménage-à-trois that lasts for decades.

Witty, elegant, stylishly photographed in color, and painstakingly detailed in sets and costumes, the film is hardly a disaster. But it does move uncertainly from the dignified to the eccentric, from utter seriousness to zany slapstick, from sentiment to cynicism, from nostalgic romanticism to anti-romantic parody. Newman and Loren are never sure whether their love scenes are serious or farcical, and the result looks like bad acting. Similarly, the character's anarchism

is alternately serious and ridiculous, and Newman, not knowing what to do, plays it in an odd contemporary style, making him appear detached and uncommitted at the same time he is supposedly dedicated and idealistic. Consequently, the critics said Newman was miscast.

Clearly, Newman's career was not being enhanced by his recent roles. He needed a critical success—and, fortunately, along came *Harper* (1966), one of his best received (and most popular) films. He returned to Warners for the first time since 1959, saying: "A feud should live a full and colorful life and then it should die a natural death and be forgotten." For Newman that was easy, because he was now a big star, and could command a high salary and a percentage of the profits. Reportedly, he also asked for a title change: the film was based on Ross MacDonald's *The Moving Target*, a Lew Archer detective novel; Newman had been so lucky with "H" titles that Archer was renamed Harper.

As the credits appear, we see Harper, unshaven and gradually awakening from a hangover. He puts his head under a faucet, attempts to make coffee but finds none left, and wearily, disgustedly, takes yesterday's grounds from the garbage and makes a perfectly horrible cup of coffee. Immediately we see this is not the glamorous world of James Bond, and we have the outline of Harper's image as the anti-heroic, boozing, slightly worn private eye. As he searches the dregs of Los Angeles for a missing multimillionaire, the details are filled in: he's tough, sardonic, cool, flip, nasty. Although occasionally given to a moment of sensitivity or remorse, he's mostly sadistic and exploitative. His philosophy: "The bottom is loaded with nice people—only cream and bastards rise."

The critics acclaimed Newman as the new Bogart, which the film encourages with its *Big Sleep* borrowings: the tortuously complicated mystery, with its many red herrings; the nighttime Southern California milieu, with its odd assortment of grotesques; the brutality, cynicism and black comedy; the appearance of Lauren Bacall herself—now a pure bitch instead of a likable cynic. Like Bogart, Harper is a loner, with an air of detachment and an ability to dispatch opponents with a fist and a wisecrack. But Bogart operated from a moral code, and when he finally committed himself, he became a chivalrous hero. Harper remains an anti-hero, disengaged morally and emotionally. He swings into action only mechanically, and does his job only because he seems to enjoy wallowing in filth.

More importantly, *The Big Sleep* was less about solving a mystery than about the Bogart-Bacall relationship, which, despite its tough veneer of cynicism and sly sexual repartee, had an underlying mutual respect, even tenderness. Harper's dealings with women are based solely on coldness, deception and sexual exploitation. He does attempt verbal playfulness with his estranged wife (Janet Leigh), but it's all done over the phone, and it's one-sided. There's no real feeling between them: he just convinces himself that he loves her, and she hates his guts.

HARPER (1966). As Lew Harper.

Therefore Harper has no saving graces, which would make sense if we were meant to condemn the amoral anti-hero, but director Jack Smight, scriptwriter William Goldman and Newman constantly attempt to enlist our support for him. Right after he walks out on his wife, he has one of many scenes in which he cleverly humiliates the befuddled cops, and we are supposed to applaud his cruel wit. Thus the film makes points about our dirty society and its heroes, then passes everything off in wisecracks. We are asked to like Harper because he's "cool." There's none of the depth, charm or vulnerability that made Ben Quick, Fast Eddie—and Bogey—so appealing. Newman resorts to externals: he chews gum endlessly, gives sidelong glances, looks around in a bored manner, makes little disapproving gestures, laughs contemptuously, grins, mugs, amuses himself with his cleverness. He pretends he's a hick, or a Graziano-style hood, or a loving husband, and it's all a giant put-on. After paying lip service to the Bogart myth, the film gives us someone not much different from James Bond after all, which is rather distasteful.

Next, in Alfred Hitchcock's *Torn Curtain* (1966), Newman plays an American nuclear scientist who pretends to defect to East Germany, so that he can trick a scientist into re-vealing a missile formula. His bewildered, abandoned fiancee (Julie Andrews) follows to see what he's up to. Not wishing to involve her, he lets her think he's a traitor, but when her confusion jeopardizes his position, he tells her the truth. Overjoyed, she helps him, and they end up in a series of chases and escapes.

The combination of Hitchcock, Andrews (fresh from *The Sound of Music*) and Newman made the film an even bigger hit than *Harper*, which had opened two months earlier. But the critics found it trite, boring and unbelievable. Newman himself dismisses the film, saying that he had been so anxious to work for Hitchcock that he took the part without reading the script. The two men did not get along, and Hitchcock, in this explanation of why he eliminated a scene, provides a revealing insight: "I wasn't too happy with the way Paul Newman had played it . . . he found it hard to just give me one of those neutral looks I needed to cut from his point of view. Instead of simply looking . . . he played the scene in the 'method' style, with emotion, and he was always turning away . . . "* Thus the inevitable conflict between an extremely manipulative director, who once called actors "cattle," and an actor who searches for motivation

*François Truffaut, *Hitchcock*, Simon & Schuster, 1971, p. 235.

TORN CURTAIN (1966). As Michael Armstrong.

TORN CURTAIN (1966). With Julie Andrews.

and is not easily pliable.

Nevertheless, Newman does come across as unemotional, or at least not very warm; in fact, critics complained that he was too intense and sullen in a part that they thought required humor. But coldness and seriousness are actually essential to the character and to Hitchcock's conception. Initially, we are supposed to share Andrews' alienation from him. Later, when we learn that he's not a traitor, we may want to view him differently, but immediately afterward he commits a gruesome killing, of a

most likable villain, which again distances us from him. From that point, even though he's apparently the "hero," his actions are never purely motivated. His attitude toward Andrews is indicative: by following him, she endangers herself, which concerns him slightly, but she also endangers the mission, which is what really troubles him.

Hitchcock, therefore, is portraying an anti-hero—not a glamorous spy, patriotically following his country's orders, or an innocent, sympathetic victim (Cary Grant in *North by Northwest*), but a man on

99

TORN CURTAIN (1966). With David Opatoshu and Julie Andrews.

his own, deliberately pursuing a selfish goal (the formula might get him back his job). Newman is thus well-cast: his indifferent rejection of the woman, his ruthlessness, his willingness to endanger lives and engender chaos, are familiar aspects of the Newman image. Here, since there isn't the balance of charm, humor or self-realization, he is un-involving. The "neutral" emotion may serve Hitchcock's plan, but it leaves the audience out in the cold.

However, this film makes him look almost excessively charming compared with *Hombre* (1967), where individualism and self-reliance lead to a complete loss of humanity. John Russell has no emo-tion (except anger) and little vitality; he's totally alienated from mankind and is *alienating* as well. Russell is a white man raised by the Indians, who call him "Hombre," and with whom he identifies. Choosing to isolate himself from white society, which he despises, he lives on a re-servation and looks and dresses like an Indian. But he's persuaded to cut his hair and return to civilization to take over some property. He winds up on a stagecoach with white passengers, who, learning his background, force him to ride with the driver. Not quite an Indian, and ostracized by whites, he's the classic outcast in no man's land. Ironically, Russell is the only one capable of rescuing the passengers from bandits and guiding them back to civilization. The drama hinges on whether he will accept responsibility for his fellow man.

Hombre, which reunited Newman with the *Hud* team (director Ritt, writers Ravetch and Frank, cinematographer Howe), resembles John Ford's classic Western, *Stagecoach*: several people, whose personal crises are outlined, are thrown together, and their interactions provide a social commentary on avarice, bigotry and responsibility. But in Ford's film, those deemed worthless by society reveal their inherent nobility, and only one man, the absconding banker, is bad. Here, the absconder—Favor (Fredric March), an Indian agent who's stolen from the Indians—is not much worse than the others. Except for Jessie (Diane Cilento), an honest, earthy woman in the Patricia Neal-*Hud* vein, they're all

HOMBRE (1967). With Diane Cilento.

HOMBRE (1967).
As John Russell.

HOMBRE (1967). With Martin Balsam.

helpless, cowardly or selfish.

In this context, Russell is an inversion of the John Wayne hero. He's strong and silent in the traditional manner, but instead of being the expected virile defender of the weak, he helps the others only when his own survival is at stake. He refuses to intercede when the malevolent bandit Grimes (Richard Boone) deprives a soldier of his seat; is willing to leave the helpless passengers stranded; indifferently sends Favor out into the desert without water ("What am I permitted to take with me?" "Your life,

how's that?"); and declines to rescue Favor's Indian-hating wife (Barbara Rush), left by the bandits to bake in the sun.

Even though he acts out of a justifiable outrage, Russell is not meant to be a sympathetic character: the white man's mistreatment may have made him indifferently cruel, but cruel he is, nevertheless. Perhaps to soften our attitude, the filmmakers have him suddenly abandon his disengagement at the end, and perform the traditional act, sacrificing himself to rescue Favor's wife. This seems arbitrary and out of charac-

COOL HAND LUKE (1967). As Luke.

COOL HAND LUKE (1967). With George Kennedy.

ter, unless it is seen as the act of a man who has stoically accepted that life is hopeless, whether one commits one's self or not. He deliberately defies the bandits by not bringing them money in exchange for the woman. As Grimes is about to kill him, he asks: "Well, now —what do you suppose hell is gonna look like?" Russell replies: "We all die—it's just a question of when." His decision (and martyrdom) seem suicidal, not heroic.

Newman's performance here is unlike any of his others. His style has been stripped away to the bare essentials; to call it underplaying would be an understatement. He imparts a sense of transcendent stillness; when he acts he does so suddenly, returning immediately thereafter to his relatively immobile state. He speaks laconically, in clipped sentences, with a solemn, deliberately monotonous, almost lifeless voice. In addition, his facial expression hardly changes; at times it approaches an infinitesimal smile, but otherwise it is sullen, grim, bitter, or inscrutably neutral.

At first glance, it seems that Newman is hardly acting, and some

COOL HAND LUKE (1967). With George Kennedy and Lou Antonio.

critics called him wooden. But one is reminded of Keaton's deadpan, which rather than being emotionless, implied an intense, inwardly directed emotion. Russell's inscrutable expression is a mask to cover his ingrained hurt, and suggests a man in a constant state of meditation or deep reflection on the chaos around him. Appropriately, the film opens and closes on close-ups of his face, and throughout, our attention is directed toward the blue eyes, which are constantly watching, thinking, judging, condemning.

Newman also frequently folds his arms as if protecting or insulating himself from the world—a natural defense mechanism of someone who's suffered a great deal of pain, and a physical equivalent of his psychological introversion. This is Newman's most completely self-sufficient, isolated, and inhuman loner, and he gives a performance that boldly risks complete alienation of the audience. And that's what happens; as in *Torn Curtain*, the character is ultimately non-involving. But it's an extremely interesting piece of disciplined acting.

106

Newman is again a cynical loner in *Cool Hand Luke* (1967), but he's also charming, and everything is calculated to involve us with him; like *Hombre*, the film begins and ends with closeups of his face, but here, appropriately, he has an engaging smile. The opening, where he drinks beer, unscrews tops from parking meters and mumbles to the arriving cop, recalls Dean's drunken incoherence at the start of *Rebel Without a Cause*—an apt title for Luke. He breaks rules for no apparent reason, wherever he is, including the chain gang to which he's sentenced. Unlike Paul Muni in *I Am a Fugitive From a Chain Gang* (1932), who steals only to eat and is turned by society into a hardened criminal, Luke is a criminal from the start. And his crime isn't motivated by hunger. It's a meaningless anti-authority gesture—the existentialist "gratuitous act," committed purely for the sake of committing it. Luke engages our sympathy not because he is economically deprived or the product of an unhappy home, but because for him the act of rebellion is its own justification: he's the perfect sixties hero.

Initially, Luke alienates the prisoners by his indifference and sarcasm, and the top dog, Dragline (George Kennedy) picks a fight with him. Luke is severely beaten but keeps fighting, and this—plus his continual defiance of the guards

—wins him the men's respect. Their admiration grows when he proves he can eat fifty eggs in an hour, another gratuitous act ("somethin' to do"). But Luke gradually becomes a victim of the adulation, rebelling because they expect him to, which leads to a pattern of escapes and captures. As the warden says, "What we got here is a failure to communicate. Some men you just can't reach." Even though Luke becomes subservient after torture, he again escapes. Dragline admires the way he fooled the guards while planning all along to escape. But Luke says he really did break down, and asserts: "I never planned anything in my life." Even his last act—shouting the "failure to communicate" line at the guards with defiant sarcasm, causing them to kill him—is motivated not by heroism but by impulse.

It's also the culmination of Luke's implied death-wish. The physical punishment Newman's characters often undergo reaches an extreme here, as Luke constantly invites pain (in his fight with Dragline, he says, "You're gonna have to kill me."). Underlying his sometimes vigorous rebelliousness is despair at a cruelly indifferent world. But the men need a hero, and Dragline perpetuates the myth, telling them that he had "that Luke smile" to the very end. We last see a montage of shots of

Luke smiling—the men's vision of him as unbeaten and almost immortal. Like Hombre, Luke becomes, in his almost suicidal act of hopeless defiance, an unwilling martyr.

Newman claimed this script was the best he'd read in years, and he approached the part enthusiastically, even to the extent of toughening his physique, getting used to walking in chains, and spending time in the Appalachian region where the film is set. His performance is among his best, and Luke is one of his definitive studies of nonconformism. As in *Hombre*, he underplays, but in a loose, relaxed, "cool" manner. He's affecting in a wide range of moods: quiet detachment, wry contempt, raw courage, exhaustion, exuberance, gentleness, anger, resignation. There's a superbly understated scene in which Luke's dying mother (Jo Van Fleet) visits him. Like Rocky Graziano, he says he tried to live cleanly, but could never find a way. But the mood is quite different here: instead of intense emotion, there are only subtle expressions of uneasiness, regret, sadness, acceptance. Newman conveys his unspoken affection entirely through his glances and reactions, as she wistfully remarks that she once had high hopes for him.

The actor even survives the film's pretentious attempts to make him a mock-Christ figure. Besides the obvious sacrifice-resurrection parallel, he's even shown in the exact crucifixion position following his fifty-egg (Last Supper?) ordeal. There are two badly conceived dialogues with a God he doesn't believe in—after which he realizes, "I gotta find my own way," a rather overt statement of existential despair—but Newman performs them with quiet conviction. His mock religion is better suggested by the bottle opener he wears in lieu of a religious medal. And the despair is effectively dramatized in his reaction to his mother's death. The men leave him by himself, and he sits on his bed, playing the banjo. With a sad, breaking voice, he sings a religious parody: "I don't care if it rains or freezes, long as I got my plastic Jesus . . . " He looks down and begins crying, but sings faster, obsessively, withdrawing into himself and expressing his utter loneliness in a world that has no God. It's one of the most moving scenes in all of Newman's work.

For *Luke*, he received his fourth Oscar nomination, but lost to Rod Steiger *(In the Heat of the Night)*. George Kennedy, however, did win the award for his supporting performance. It was Newman's fourth consecutive box-office success, and he received the Hollywood Foreign Press Association's Golden Globe

THE SECRET WAR OF HARRY FRIGG (1968). With Sylva Koscina.

Award as the World's Favorite Actor.

His next film, *The Secret War of Harry Frigg* (1968), a painfully familiar, styleless farce, was a large step backward. Newman's second film for Jack Smight, it was his first "service comedy"—the kind that tells us World War II and prison camps were really fun. Newman plays Private Frigg, a character superficially similar to Luke: a rebel and consummate escape artist who lands perpetually in the stockade. When five Allied generals are captured, and prove reluctant to escape from the luxurious Italian villa that is their prison, Frigg is promoted to Major General, and is sent in to lead them out. But once at the villa, he falls for the beautiful owner (Sylva Koscina), and keeps delaying the escape.

Frigg turns out to be another Rocky Graziano: the same poor New York background, the same

THE SECRET WAR OF HARRY FRIGG (1968). Frigg and the generals escape from prison.

propensity for winding up at the bottom (and in prison). And Newman uses the Graziano mannerisms: the New York accent, the half-idiotic mumble, the hunched shoulders and fidgety walk, the rubbing, scratching, and pouting. He even imports several of Rocky's lines. Newman is often amusing as the boor and goof-off who must pass himself off as a cultured general, and who constantly feels uncomfortable and out of his element. But too often Newman himself seems uncomfortable, and he overdoes the comedy in his usual manner. He ~s, postures and does the whole

Rocky routine with a self-consciousness and fakery that make it all seem forced. Frigg is a badly conceived character to begin with—too modern and sixties-cool for the period—and the film itself is never certain whether it's a fantasy, escape thriller or serious statement about role-playing.

Newman says he did *Frigg* because he thought he might have fun with the character, and because "an actor has to work." It was becoming extremely difficult to find worthwhile scripts: "Motion pictures today are in as bad shape as the theater, in terms of really distinguished pieces of writing. If I waited until I got a good script, I would work about once every three years."* But this obviously meant appearing in too many inferior films, which bothered him, especially since he thought that even in his best work he was becoming uncreative: "When you get to be around forty, it's very necessary to make a break, or to effect some kind of wrench in your life . . . I find that I've been repeating myself in performances, and in judgments, because I'm burned out creatively. I can't invent anymore. I've done it."**

It was clearly time for a change, and when the right project came along, Newman made a decision —one that proved extremely fortunate. He was ready to direct his first feature.

* Richard Warren Lewis, "Paul Newman Makes a Western," *New York Times Magazine*, November 6, 1966.

** Jane Wilson, "What if My Eyes Turn Brown?", *Saturday Evening Post*, February 24, 1968.

For Newman, who considers himself such a "cerebral" actor, directing was a logical step: "I've always wanted to direct because I've always enjoyed most the peripheral things about acting, the rehearsals and the field trips, the exploration of character and the whole intellectual exercise of the thing. I enjoy this more than actually getting up on a stage or in front of a camera. That has always been more painful to me than enjoyable. I guess I've never been that much of an exhibitionist."*

Although everyone spoke of *Rachel, Rachel* as his first film, Newman had directed (and independently produced) a black-and-white, 28-minute short, *On the Harmfulness of Tobacco*, in 1961. Based on a Chekhov play, it consists almost entirely of a man (Michael Strong) delivering a lecture which is supposed to be on the dangers of tobacco, but which keeps turning into a complaint about his shrewish wife. Strong's delivery, like Newman's in some films, is humorously dry and understated. Newman employs harsh contrasts of light and dark, creating an eerie, expressionistic atmosphere, and he shows versatility with his camera—panning, dollying, and cutting to various angles as the man speaks.

*Jane Wilson; "What if My Eyes Turn Brown?"

NEW DIRECTIONS

However, the technique never overshadows the performance, something rare in a first film (although not surprising, since Newman is an actor). He has said, about his later films, that he makes the camera follow the actors, not the reverse, and it is evident here. The camera is used to explore character, and to help develop the man from an absurd fool into a pathetic human being. We are fully involved with him near the end, when in closeup he says, "How I long not to remember," and Newman pulls away, leaving him in stark solitude. *Tobacco* is a tour-de-force in which Newman, aided by Strong's subtle performance, accomplishes what has eluded many more experienced directors: a filmed monologue that is neither stagy nor overwhelmed by distracting technique.

Although the film had only a brief art-house run, Newman said, "It was the best creative experience I've ever had. I was just absolutely alive." He wanted to direct again, and over six years later decided to take the chance. His wife discovered Margaret Laurence's novel, *A Jest of God*, and their friend, screenwriter Stewart Stern (*The Rack*), began working on a script.

112

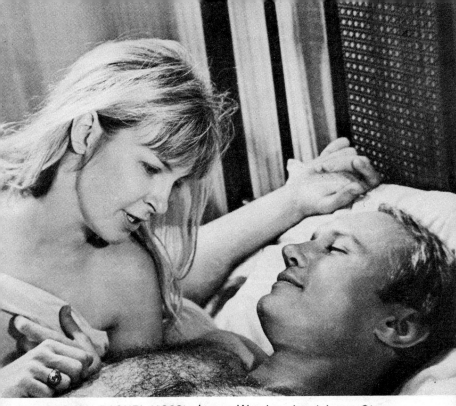

RACHEL, RACHEL (1968). Joanne Woodward and James Olson.

They persuaded Newman to produce it, and as discussions took place, he gradually became interested in directing as well. But even with his name, it was difficult to raise money, because the subject was considered uncommercial. After many companies turned him down, Warners, his old alma mater, gave him $700,000. He was able to make the film (retitled *Rachel, Rachel*) on such a small budget by taking no salaries for himself and Woodward, and by filming it in five weeks in Danbury, Conn. It became a real family project: his brother Arthur was co-producer and the Newmans' oldest daughter, Elinor ("Nell Potts"), played Rachel as a child.

In a variation on her *Long Hot Summer* role, Woodward plays a plain, repressed schoolteacher in a small New England town who realizes that life is passing her by: she is thirty-five, a virgin, and dominated by her mother. During the summer, she has an affair with

113

RACHEL, RACHEL (1968). Joanne Woodward as Rachel.

an old schoolmate. It proves disappointing, but she now knows that she can be loving, and determines to leave town and do something about her life—a move that seems only tentatively hopeful.

What might have been a sentimental soap opera becomes a gentle, richly emotional, melancholy (but, amazingly, never depressing) experience. Newman shows a natural cinematic sense in his perceptive depictions of small town life, the frenzied activity of a revival meeting and the anxieties of a first sexual experience; and in his subtle, rarely obtrusive juxtaposition of Rachel's present with her fantasies and childhood memories. He gets excellent performances from Estelle Parsons as another lonely teacher and James Olson as the cynical big-city man who lets Rachel down (a Newman role played in Newman style).

The film, however, belongs to Woodward, giving her finest performance as the confused, awkward, constantly beaten but ultimately indestructible woman. She has an extraordinary ability to look natural or plain and still reveal an inner radiance. There are many touching moments: her nervousness at the religious meeting; her clumsiness with the man; her late-night discussion with a sympathetic male friend; and, most unforgettable, her face turning from joyous

expectancy to barely suppressed hysteria to a painful outburst of tears when she learns that, contrary to her hopes, she is not pregnant.

The film was shot in the summer of 1967, but was not released until the following August. It was, surprisingly, an enormous success, grossing over $8 million, and appearing on more critics' ten best lists than any other film except *The Lion in Winter*. Both Newman and Woodward won Golden Globe Awards. In addition, she won the coveted New York Film Critics' Award, and was nominated for an Oscar, as were Parsons, Stern and the film itself. But although Newman also won the New York Film Critics' Award, often an indication of the eventual Oscar winner, Hollywood chose to deny him even a nomination for his directing.

His apparent unpopularity in certain Hollywood circles may be due to his continual anti-Hollywood remarks, but more likely, it results from his well-known political activities. In 1968, Newman was the first show-business personality to endorse Eugene McCarthy, and he took time out from his editing of *Rachel* to campaign for the Senator extensively in New Hampshire, Indiana, Wisconsin and other states. He and Frank Perry produced a 25-minute film on the New Hampshire campaign, with profits going to the candidate. That summer, he

RACHEL, RACHEL (1968). Rachel at the tabernacle meeting.

was a Connecticut delegate to the Democratic convention in Chicago.

Newman's political involvement had begun as far back as the Stevenson ('56) and Kennedy campaigns, but he became deeply committed from 1964 on, speaking out frequently against the Vietnam War. He also participated in many civil rights demonstrations, including the 1963 March on Washington, a fair housing sit-in in Sacramento and a community understanding rally led by Dr. Martin Luther King in Gadsden, Alabama. In some of these he was alongside Marlon Brando.

In 1970, he worked for Joseph Duffy, liberal candidate for the Democratic Senatorial nomination in Connecticut, and in 1972, he supported Rep. Paul N. McCloskey's fight against Nixon in the Republican primaries, and was one of Senator McGovern's leading show business supporters. Newman once asserted, in 1967: "People in Hollywood come up to me and say: 'Why take a chance? Don't make enemies. It can't possibly help you.'

My reaction is: 'Kiss off.' I still have my citizenship papers. Did I lose them when I became an actor? Do I just abdicate? What they're basically asking me to do is be a person without character. A person without character has no enemies. So I prefer to make enemies."

In this he has succeeded. At the Senate's Watergate Hearings in June 1973, former Nixon counsel John W. Dean released the so-called White House "Political Enemies" list, compiled in mid-1971. On the list of the twenty original "priority" names was only one performer: Paul Newman. He was described as follows: "Radic-lib causes. Heavy McCarthy involvement '68. Used effectively in nationwide TV commercials. '72 involvement uncertain." Newman "accepted" his honor with an irony worthy of Hud: "I am sending Gordon Liddy to pick up my award. I would like to thank John Mitchell, Jeb Magruder, John Dean 3d and Maurice Stans for making this award possible."

Back in 1968, following Rachel's success, Newman received other offers to direct, but he waited for the right script. In the meantime, he and his agent John Foreman formed the Newman-Foreman Company, the first production of which was Winning (1969). Director James Goldstone says that Newman, after his intense work on Rachel,

"wanted to have fun, wanted to race cars and make a lot of money for doing it." The last was certainly true: he received $1.1 million, his highest salary thus far, plus a percentage of the profits for his company. Winning had been planned as a TV movie, with a story built around footage Universal owned of the 1968 Indianapolis 500. But once Newman was signed, it kept growing until it was a $7 million theatrical feature (which used only forty seconds of the original footage).

Goldstone says: "It was really his picture all the way. I was in no position to tamper with Paul's image, nor did I want to." This is apparent in the plot. Newman is a successful driver who marries a small-town divorcée (Joanne Woodward), soon after they've met. As usual, he devotes too much time to his career and ignores everything else, and, as in From the Terrace, Woodward turns in desperation to another man—here a rival driver (Robert Wagner). Newman finds them in bed, and becomes estranged from her (again, as in Terrace), but after winning the big race, he realizes his life is empty, and attempts a reconciliation (the theme of the "winner" who's really a loser).

The relationship is superficially written, but Newman and Woodward make us care about it. Their first film together since A New Kind of Love, it's their best since The

117

WINNING (1969). As Frank Capua.

WINNING (1969). With Joanne Woodward.

Long Hot Summer. They exude a
naturalness, intimacy and spontaneous affection that one suspects
come from their own feelings for
each other. It is apparent in their
first scene, where he is slightly
drunk, delightfully playful, and confident (but no longer obnoxious) in
his attempt to pick her up; and she
responds with smiles and applause
at his tricks with a fireman's hat, but
looks slightly uncertain about this
glamorous stranger. Following
their wedding, they sit on a swing,
drinking beer from cans, talking and

laughing quietly. She describes her
previous loneliness, and he responds, typically, "Beer's a lot less
complicated." They smile, she rubs
his back and leans her head on his
shoulder: these are people who really know each other, and who have
attained a maturity about themselves.

Newman exhibits this maturity
throughout. His loose, casual style,
evident in *Cool Hand Luke,* has
given way to an almost complete
mellowness. Perhaps because of the
confidence gained from his direct-

BUTCH CASSIDY AND THE SUNDANCE KID (1969). With Katharine Ross and Robert Redford.

ing experience, he has gotten rid of his mannerisms; and except for the intense determination he shows while racing, he's more relaxed than ever before. Although the script tells little about his past, there's a wealth of experience etched into his face, especially in his brilliant, silent reaction to finding the couple in bed—one of quiet resignation that suggests a lifetime of pain and frustration. He has many fine scenes of quiet underplaying: his camaraderie with Wagner early in the film; his solitude after the race; his genuine warmth in the relationship with his stepson (Richard Thomas). The scenes in which they drink champagne and come home drunk together project for the first time in Newman's career a really paternal feeling—only vaguely suggested in strikingly similar scenes in *Hud*.

Newman's mellowness is abundantly evident in *Butch Cassidy and the Sundance Kid* (1969). Director George Roy Hill says: "I saw [Butch] as a warm, open, amiable guy, and that's exactly what Newman is." Because he plays an easygoing, naturally funny fellow instead of an exaggerated comic character, Newman doesn't overact, and the result is his finest comedy performance.

The turn-of-the-century outlaws are neither romanticized as in a traditional Western, nor grossly ridiculed as in most spoofs. Instead, they are seen with a humanistic irony, as men who make inept blunders, commit anti-heroic acts and engage in constant wisecracking and self-mockery. And there's an underlying sadness for two still-young men who have outlived their day.

Newman and Robert Redford clearly like each other, and this creates an immensely appealing camaraderie, which is rare in Newman's career. (His intense loners generally avoid male friendships.) The good-natured fellowship is felt from the opening—a humorous fight with a man who's accused Sundance of cheating at cards—to the final scene, in which their quiet banter is touching in the face of their imminent deaths at the hands of an entire Army regiment. In between, the warmth emerges in scenes of their train robberies, their flight from the "super posse," their almost idyllic relationship with Sundance's girl Etta (Katharine Ross), their escape to Bolivia, their abortive attempt to go straight.

Sundance is closer to the traditional Western character: strong, silent, dead-pan, willing to face confrontations and shoot it out. Butch is an atypical outlaw: he's enormously charming and affable, has never killed anyone, and tries to avoid showdowns. Butch has the best comic moments, as when he tries to con-

BUTCH CASSIDY AND THE SUNDANCE KID (1969).
With Robert Redford.

vince Sundance to jump off a cliff into a stream so they can avoid the posse. Sundance confesses he can't swim, and Butch says, "You stupid fool, the fall'll probably kill you." In their robbery of a Bolivian bank, he gets confused with his newly-learned Spanish and must refer to crib sheets to give instructions. And in the famous "Raindrops Keep Fallin'" scene, Butch gives Etta a ride on his bicycle, then jokes and performs acrobatic tricks in a refreshing, improvisatory manner. Throughout the film, Newman is

engagingly spontaneous in his expressions, gestures and timing of dialogue.

Whereas Sundance is practical, Butch is a hopelessly ridiculous optimist and romantic dreamer—a humorous version of Newman's seekers of impossible goals. He keeps saying, "I got vision and the rest of the world wears bifocals." His vision of riches in Bolivia turns into a nightmare, but even as they are facing death he plans for their future in Australia, the "latest in a long line" of great ideas. While they flee the posse, he continually expresses optimism, but beneath is a child-like need for reassurance. He says: "I think we lost 'em. Do you think we lost 'em?" Sundance: "No." Butch: "Neither do I." Small indications of his self-awareness emerge at other times, undercutting his casual exterior. For instance, despite the naturalness of the *ménage-à-trois*, Butch is really the outsider, and he knows it. In the lovely still-photo montage of their New York holiday, Butch watches with wistful longing as they dance, but then smiles—aware of his isolation but content in their happiness.

The film received mixed reviews, and one can easily object to its liberal borrowings from other films, especially *Bonnie and Clyde;* its anachronistic contemporary sensibility; its casual attitude toward violence and its superficial, "hip" cleverness. (Scriptwriter William Goldman also wrote *Harper.*) But it was also one of the most entertaining films in years, and it appealed to a huge audience, grossing over $30 million. And although Newman was

BUTCH CASSIDY AND THE SUNDANCE KID (1969).
With Robert Redford.

WUSA (1970). As Rheinhardt.

better playing a more fully developed character like Fast Eddie, he never gave a more relaxed performance.

In October, 1969, Newman-Foreman paid $500,000 for the rights to Arthur Kopit's play *Indians*, with Newman scheduled to do the Buffalo Bill role originated by Stacy Keach, and George Roy Hill to direct, but it fell through. That month, Newman made an infrequent television appearance, as narrator-host of *From Here to the Seventies*, a 2½-hour NBC News show exploring "America now and in the future." The producer selected him because "he is a representative of the times . . . an involved, concerned citizen."

Newman's concern is again demonstrated in *WUSA* (1970), which he calls "the most significant film I've ever made and probably the best," and which was the only film he ever promoted through extensive personal appearances. The critics were much less enthusiastic, and the film, which cost $4.8 million, was hardly shown in the U.S.; thus, from his biggest hit, he went to his biggest flop. Newman bitterly blamed audiences' unwillingness to face the truth. (Ironically, that would confirm the film's very thesis about public apathy.)

The idea that a super-patriotic New Orleans radio station (WUSA) could become the vanguard of a right-wing plot to take over the U.S. was dismissed by critics as liberal paranoia. Today, smugness isn't so easy, considering the institutionalized conspiracies and crimes masked by law-and-order appeals, and sanctioned by massive apathy, in recent years. But the film still suffers from conversations that sound like speeches, heavy-handed direction by Stuart Rosenberg (*Cool Hand Luke*), and a paradoxical reluctance really to meet the issues head-on (WUSA's anti-welfare scheme, which occupies much of the plot, is obliquely depicted, and even the station's ultimate objective is only hinted at).

Perhaps because the drama is so overwrought, Newman's subtle underplaying is effective. Rheinhardt is his most thorough cynic: a failure at marriage and as a musician, he's become a wandering, alcoholic opportunist, so spineless and corrupt he thinks nothing of taking a job as announcer for WUSA. At last—a Newman character who's abandoned all ideals, ambitions and principles, who concentrates solely on surviving at all costs. He's even worse than Hud, because he realizes his corruption but persists. In fact, he uses his self-knowledge to pretend superiority—to laugh secretly at the neo-Fascists, while working for them. He acts cynically and viciously toward liberal do-gooders because presumably he

WUSA (1970). With Joanne Woodward.

"knows the score," although he really envies their idealism; and he rises above it all to a liquor-soaked detachment. His sole ability is the put-on—once the essence of Harper's charm, now exposed as the weapon of a destructive mind.

Rheinhardt's first appearance —he drifts into New Orleans, unshaven, tired, defeated, broke —is like Fast Eddie's after his loss to Fats, but now Newman really looks world-weary; even in later films he isn't quite so jowly. Like Eddie, he picks up a despairing, fallen woman, Geraldine (Joanne Woodward), a former hooker who, like Sarah, is physically and emotionally scarred. As always, Woodward flawlessly portrays the fragile, easily hurt woman who is wary of Newman, but who ends up giving him more affection than he can return. They have some tender scenes, but with her, as with everyone else, he's mostly indifferent and uninvolved.

He resists her love and questioning of his values, retreats into the world of his whiskey-filled thermos bottle and sardonic contempt, and eventually leaves her. Even his thorough self-awareness never redeems him. At the climactic WUSA patriotic rally to kick off its campaign, Rheinhardt, the m.c., becomes drunk and detached. Chaos results from an assassination attempt, and as people run in panic, he delivers a sarcastic speech with all the right-wing cliches, again proving to himself his smug superiority. The distraught Geraldine winds up in jail, and, like Sarah, kills herself in despair.

When Rheinhardt hears about this, he shows more involvement than at at any other time, reacting with stunned silence, closing his eyes and looking away in pain, holding back his tears—but it's nothing like Eddie's agony. He visits her grave, then leaves town, telling his neighbor, "I was out there—it's sad." The man replies, "Don't worry, Rheinhardt, everything's dying." Rheinhardt looks back at him (and toward us) and says, "Not me—I'm a survivor. Ain't that great?" The frame freezes on his look of weary disgust. He's affected by what his apathy has caused, but unlike Eddie, who becomes a human being, Rheinhardt will go on, aware of his rottenness but unable to change.

Newman's next film, *Sometimes a Great Notion*, was plagued with problems. In July, 1970, three weeks after shooting had begun in Oregon, co-producer Newman fired director Richard Colla, claiming "he didn't understand the subject in the way I thought he should." To avoid delays, Newman took over as director. But soon afterward, he broke his ankle in a motorcycle accident, and shooting was postponed, bringing the film over its

SOMETIMES A GREAT NOTION (1971). As Hank Stamper.

$3.6 million budget. Editing difficulties delayed release until late 1971, and Universal was confused about how to market it, resulting in a commercial failure. This was the third Newman-Foreman flop of the year; they had also produced *They Might Be Giants*, with George C. Scott and Joanne Woodward, and *Puzzle of a Downfall Child*, with Faye Dunaway.

Notion is based on Ken Kesey's complex novel of a contemporary family of lumberjacks who stubbornly maintain 19th-century frontier values, and whose motto is "Never Give a Inch." The Stampers' patriarch, Henry (Henry Fonda), his son Hank (Newman) and nephew Joe Ben (Richard Jaeckel) alienate the entire community by refusing to participate in a local strike, because they're anti-union and want to honor their contract to deliver lumber. They overcome hostility, sabotage and violence, but succumb to nature: a falling log causes Joe to drown, and kills Henry by severing his arm. Hank's wife Viv (Lee Remick) leaves him the same day, and he goes on an alcoholic binge. But finally he decides to finish their job by floating four huge rafts of logs downstream almost singlehandedly. The strikers watch in anger and disbelief as Hank, to emphasize his defiance, ties Henry's arm to the tugboat—its middle finger extended in the familiar gesture of contempt.

Hank is another of Newman's tough, macho individualists, somewhat like Hud. He brawls, hunts, drinks beer constantly, has no social conscience, and is coldly sarcastic, especially toward the strikers and his half-brother Lee (Michael Sarrazin), a hippie with pro-union and women's lib ideas. Hank shares his father's professional pride, rigid conservatism and purpose in life: "To work and eat and sleep and screw and drink—that's all there is." The women play a marginal role, as is customary in male adventure films—they cook, clean and are passive sex objects.

Newman is dissatisfied with *Notion*: "not the kind of material I would pick to direct." One might ask why he even wanted to star in a film that invites identification with right-wing types. Of course, liberals like Newman and Henry Fonda couldn't play John Wayne characters completely straight, so occasionally they make individualism seem like plain stubbornness. But most of the time they're appealing, and the defiant ending is unmistakable: like Hud and Rheinhardt, Hank shows few regrets and goes on as before, but now we're meant to applaud the "survivor."

Despite the ideological schizophrenia, ill-defined relationships and implausible plot resolutions, the film is surprisingly stirring.

SOMETIMES A GREAT NOTION (1971). With Richard Jaeckel.

Newman says he was uncomfortable directing himself, but his performance is subtle and assured, and blends into the ensemble. He captures with zest the details of logging and the robust family life, as well as the kind of exhilarating camaraderie and professionalism that characterized the best thirties adventure films.

This extroverted, outdoors, masculine adventure contrasts sharply with the two introverted, confined, feminine dramas he has directed, but, interestingly, the combination of toughness and sensitivity consti-

tutes Newman's own screen image. Significantly, the film's highlight —Joe Ben's drowning—is an intimate drama enacted by two rugged men. As Joe is pinned by the log, Hank tries everything possible to move it, and Joe wisecracks to forget his pain. They hope that the rising tide will take the log away, but as night approaches and the water rises, nothing happens, and the joking becomes uneasy. Joe's head goes under water, and Hank gives mouth-to-mouth respiration, which Joe finds amusing. He smiles, caresses Hank's hair and—in

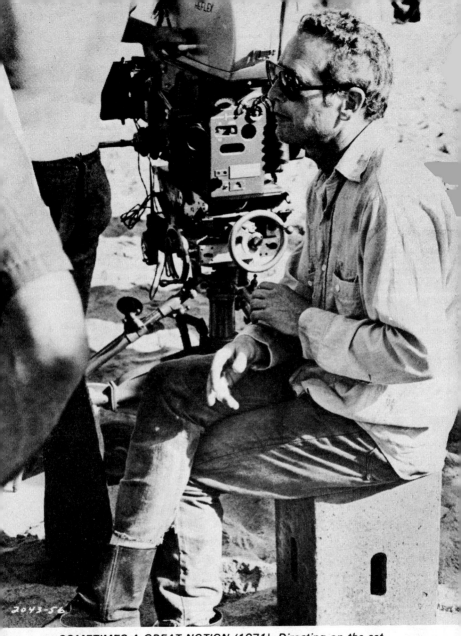

SOMETIMES A GREAT NOTION (1971). Directing on the set.

POCKET MONEY (1972). With Lee Marvin.

a horrifying instant—laughs, causing him to swallow water and drown.

The delicate balance between humor and horror, the suspenseful drawing out of time, the genuine feeling of brotherly love, the finely judged performances (Jaeckel was nominated for an Oscar), and Newman's expert use of long shots (emphasizing their utter desolation) and closeups (giving us a sense of claustrophobia) create the best scene he ever directed.

Newman had yet to make a film for the First Artists Production Company that he, Barbra Streisand and Sidney Poitier had formed in 1969 (Steve McQueen joined in 1971). Various projects were planned for 1971, including *Hillman*, in which Newman would be evicted from a house he had made of garbage, and *Where the Dark Streets Go*, in which he would play a priest. Neither was made, but they indicated his interest in new kinds of roles. He found one in *Pocket Money*, made for First Artists and released in 1972. It was his third consecutive commercial failure.

Another Stuart Rosenberg film, it's a contemporary Western comedy about Jim Kane, a good-natured, absurdly naive, overly honest, bumbling Texas cowboy who owns a pickup truck on its last wheels, is behind in alimony and bank payments, and consistently makes bad bargains. Desperate for money, he goes to Mexico to bring back cattle for a rodeo supplier who's crooked, but whom the ever-trusting Jim likes. He does everything wrong, so his old pal Leonard (Lee Marvin) decides to help him. Leonard's the opposite type: a showy, crafty, fancy-pants dude who dreams of getting rich, considers himself an authority on Mexicans and hustles everyone in sight. He convinces Kane that they can swindle the Mexicans, but turns out to be equally inefficient, and the two lose all their money.

An extremely low-key, leisurely-paced fable, with long pauses between actions and sentences, *Pocket Money* is appropriately dry for Newman's mellow period. He deliberately works against his image; never before has he played such an ingenuous and inept loser. Speaking with a high, nasal drawl, acting like an adolescent, looking constantly bewildered and wearing jeans that make him look bowlegged, he's rather funny if occasionally self-conscious. Marvin's part, with its broad, loud comedy, is showier; Newman mostly behaves quietly and tosses out flip lines. At one point he is more animated, and irately tosses a TV set out of a motel window to get back at a man who's cheated them. It's the new Western's equivalent of the old Western's cathartic showdown at high noon—a perfect, anti-heroic act of a modern anti-hero.

Newman returned to the Old West in John Huston's *The Life and Times of Judge Roy Bean (1972)*, but it's another anti-heroic, comic Western. Bean rides into Vinegar-roon, Texas in 1890, and is promptly beaten, robbed and hanged by degenerate outlaws and whores. The rope breaks, and he returns, shooting everyone in revenge. Then he declares himself "the Law West of the Pecos," makes the saloon his courthouse, and swears to uphold the honor of his ideal, the beautiful actress, Lily Langtry. He takes Marie, a Mexican girl (Victoria Principal), as his mistress, and administers justice by hanging men and confiscating their property to make the town (renamed Langtry) prosperous. Eventually, the community turns against him, and Bean—his Marie having died after childbirth—rides out, defeated.

Twenty years later, in 1925, the town is run by Prohibition gangsters and evil oil men. Out of nowhere, Bean, now seventy, appears and purges the town by shooting the criminals. During the gunfight, the oil derricks catch fire, and the whole town burns down. Bean dies in

POCKET MONEY (1972). As Jim Kane.

THE LIFE AND TIMES OF JUDGE ROY BEAN (1972).
As Judge Roy Bean.

*THE LIFE AND TIMES OF JUDGE ROY BEAN (1972). On the set
with director John Huston.*

mythic glory, riding through the
flames and shouting the name of his
beloved Lily.

In a sense, Newman comes full
circle from his first Western, in
which Billy the Kid also said, "I am
the law," and fought evil by becoming judge, jury and executioner. But
whereas Billy was a neurotic, pitiful
adolescent, Bean is presented as an
admirable, manly primitive. The
real Bean died in 1903, and scriptwriter John Milius presumably
changed the date in order to contrast the rugged individualist with
impersonal twenties gangsters:
even though he's a killer, he does it
with style. The film tries to make
Bean another lovable character on
the order of Butch Cassidy: he
hangs and shoots men while quoting

the Bible and delivering wisecracks, and he punctuates their
deaths with punch lines. (A man killed by Bean's deputies is fined for
"lying around".)

Newman—his voice gruff, his delivery dry and deadpan—does his
best with the material. His funniest
scenes are with a huge bear named
Bruno, who, like Bean, is grizzly,
guzzles beer and deals violently
with outlaws; at one point he delightfully evokes Bean's wrath by
drunkenly licking Lily's poster. In
1940's *The Westerner*, Walter
Brennan as Bean upstaged Gary
Cooper; here Bruno upstages
Newman. In any case, the outrageous gallows humor and broad
caricatures fail to disguise the fact
that unlike Butch, Bean is a vicious

fellow. Even the other *Butch Cassidy* elements—the lyrical song interlude, still-photo montage and hip dialogue—cannot counterbalance the nasty implications, especially of Bean's final blood purge.

Because Bean is either a butcher or a buffoon, the attempts to evoke sympathy for him are mostly unsuccessful, although there's one lovely scene in which he and Marie walk at sunset, and he tells her his dreams for the town, then sings "The Yellow Rose of Texas." When she dies, there is pathos as Bean, realizing his love too late, hugs her and yells in anguish. But immediately thereafter, he tries to hang the doctor who failed to arrive in time, and we're again alienated. Symptomatic of the film's perversity is that the bear's death is more moving. Bean's only affecting trait is his lifelong devotion to Lily, whom he never meets—a rare instance of Newman placing a woman on a pedestal (although of course she's only a distant vision, another of Newman's unattainable goals, and Marie, the reality, is treated off-handedly).

The final scene, in which, years after Bean's death, the legendary Lily (personified by the legendary Ava Gardner) arrives in town to visit the museum dedicated to her, is haunting enough to redeem much of the rest. But the film is hardly a milestone for Huston, who portrayed hopeless dreamers more effectively in films like *The Treasure of the Sierra Madre* and *The Asphalt Jungle*. It was another commercial failure for Newman, although he and Huston got along so well they teamed again in 1973 for *The Mackintosh Man*.

But first, Newman directed his third feature, *The Effect of Gamma Rays on Man-in-the-Moon Marigolds* (1972), which Alvin Sargent adapted from Paul Zindel's Pulitzer Prize-winning play. Joanne Woodward starred as Beatrice Hunsdorfer ("Betty the Loon"), a loud, vulgar, gum-chewing, beer-drinking, middle-aged frump. Living in a dilapidated house in a run-down town, abandoned by her husband, unable to face the responsibility of raising her two teenaged daughters, she is disgusted with life. She covers her despair with sarcasm, outrageous jokes and a tough, insensitive treatment of the girls. But she's also pathetic, as she checks the classified ads for business opportunities, and dreams of opening dignified teashops, even though her house is filled with garbage and she's a frightful mess.

The film focuses on the way Beatrice's savage, cynical, often self-deprecating humor and her embittered outlook have affected her daughters. Ruth, the older girl, is a typical adolescent boy-chaser and baton-twirler, who, like Beatrice, employs a tough, sarcastic

THE LIFE AND TIMES OF JUDGE ROY BEAN (1972).
With Anthony Perkins.

manner to hide her fears and frustration. Shattered by nightmares and epileptic fits, she sinks hopelessly into defeat. Matilda is shy, sensitive and introverted. Although it seems that she should succumb, she overcomes her environment and emerges strongest. An extremely intelligent science student, Matilda wins a prize for her experiment on mutated flowers that gives the drama its symbolic title; and she becomes a mutant herself—a delicate flower growing out of arid waste.

The play is transformed from a lyrical mood-piece into a naturalistic slice-of-life in the tradition of the fifties television drama Newman admires. This makes the symbolism somewhat obtrusive, and the emphasis on external squalor—the filthy house, for example—is overdone and superficial. Newman's attempts to open up the play are largely successful—scenes of Matilda's science teacher explaining the mysteries of the universe, Ruth's accurate imitation of Beatrice in a school skit, and a teenaged mad scientist explaining with sadistic relish how she skinned a cat, are especially memorable. As in *Sometimes a Great Notion,* there's a real feeling for family life, although the emphasis is reversed: here it's a world of women in which men play a marginal role. Newman expertly handles the shifts from vigorous burlesque to black humor to terror to pathos. And as before, he uses the camera functionally, bringing it close to his actresses to achieve intimacy and character revelation.

Woodward again displays remarkable range. As the obnoxious virago, she's at once horrifying and humorous, but her suggestion of underlying vulnerability arouses our compassion. There's even the familiar inner radiance, indicating a beautiful woman beneath the flamboyance. As Ruth, Roberta Wallach (daughter of Eli Wallach and Anne Jackson) is a perfect amalgam of the tough, shallow teenager and the pathetic, defenseless baby. The standout performance is by Nell Potts, the Newmans' thirteen-year-old, who played Rachel as a child, and here plays a Rachel-like character. As Matilda, she's a model of understatement, with her soft, fragile voice, subtle expressions of nervousness, and luminous blue eyes that, like her father's, seem to be quietly assimilating everything —sometimes disapproving but more often understanding.

At the end, Matilda has attained a mature awareness of herself and forgiveness for her mother. As Beatrice and Ruth sit outside under

THE EFFECT OF GAMMA RAYS ON MAN-IN-THE-MOON MARIGOLDS (1972). Nell Potts as Matilda.

the night sky—the mother explaining her latest fantasy of turning the yard into a patio garden, the older daughter staring dumbly—Matilda sits serenely by herself, thinking about her experiment. The camera moves slowly toward her, as her voice-over expresses how important she feels. Earlier, Beatrice asked, "Don't you hate the world, Matilda?" Now, as her beautiful face fills the screen, she says, "No mama, I

THE EFFECT OF GAMMA RAYS ON MAN-IN-THE-MOON MARIGOLDS (1972). Nell Potts, Joanne Woodward, and Roberta Wallach.

don't hate the world." Like *Rachel*, the film ends on a note of tentative optimism, with the possibility that something vital and lovely will emerge from the darkness.

Despite generally warm reviews, *Marigolds* was not a success, perhaps because of its downbeat subject or its title, although *Rachel* had the same liabilities. But it did reconfirm Newman's stature as a director. In his three features he has shown an ability to work with a wide range of material, and if he lacks an original style, he does have a feeling for constructing powerful images and scenes. Above all, he is one of today's finest directors of performers, which has become almost a lost art.

Newman's own performance in John Huston's *The Mackintosh Man* (1973) is far from exciting. The film, in which he plays a British secret agent involved in a complex Cold War plot, is absurdly contrived, and there is little suspense or energy. Newman is as lifeless as the story. For variety, he has an automobile chase in Ireland, underwater swimming near Malta, and an occasional Australian accent. But throughout, his expression remains unchanged—it's the gray look of world-weary disgust he perfected in *WUSA*. The worst-acted scenes involve his romantic interlude with Dominique Sanda, but the relationship is superficial and pointless in the first place.

At times, Huston and Newman seem to be condemning the cold, inhuman men (and women) in espionage, but they choose to involve us with the "hero" at precisely his most reprehensible moments. The only humor consists of Newman's sexist and anti-homosexual remarks and his casual approach to violence. The film's sole catharsis occurs when Newman, having been severely beaten, gets back at his captors by batting them over their heads, setting fire to their house, and viciously kicking a woman in the groin. In *WUSA*, Newman meant us to censure the cynical mercenary, but in *Sometimes a Great Notion*, and particularly in the two Huston films, he invites us to applaud the fascist mentality, sadism, brutal vengeance or nihilism of his characters, and it's a peculiar and disheartening development in his work.

The Mackintosh Man was Newman's sixth consecutive commercial failure (including *Marigolds*); clearly his popularity had declined since *Butch Cassidy*. But with his later 1973 release, *The Sting*, he had an opportunity to regain his box-office standing. The film was an obviously calculated attempt to recapture the *Butch Cassidy* magic, which Newman badly needed at that point. He was again teamed with director George Roy Hill and Robert Redford, and the two stars again played outlaws who are basically easy-going and human, and

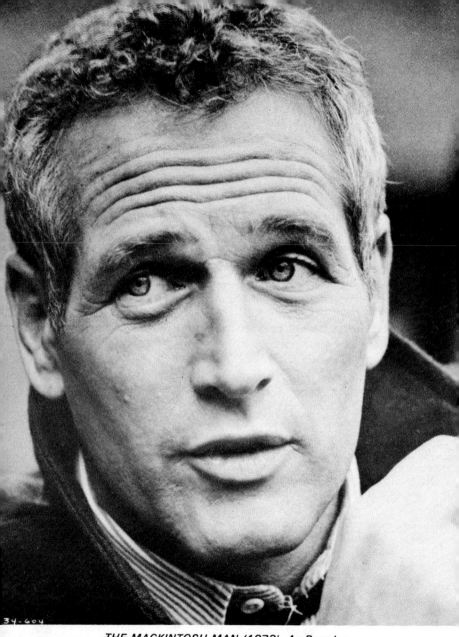

THE MACKINTOSH MAN (1973). As Rearden.

whose criminal exploits are comically engaging.

Here the setting is Chicago in 1936. Henry Gondorff (Newman), a well-known, slightly aging con artist, is hiding from the law, but he comes out of retirement to teach small-time hustler Johnny Hooker (Redford) the "Big Con." With the assistance of a large group of amiable crooks, the two work out an elaborate scheme to cheat an important racketeer, Doyle Lonnegan (Robert Shaw), out of $500,000.

Unlike *Butch Cassidy,* the film is inordinately complicated, and has many twists, turns and surprises. It is actually one con game after another, with the audience tricked as well as the characters. The steps in the swindle fall neatly into place in the manner of television's *Mission: Impossible,* although once we think about the plot, it makes little sense. But we're not meant to think; *The Sting* is designed, and works extremely well, as slick entertainment.

Gondorff, like Butch, is the "brains" of the outfit, but he is unmistakably experienced and professional, and has little need for reassurance. In fact, Hooker, who is somewhat childlike and naive, is actually closer to Butch. He also shares Butch's tendency toward idealism: his purpose in the scheme is to avenge a friend's death, whereas Gondorff does it simply because "it seems worthwhile." The pair have almost a father-son relationship (Gondorff continually calls Hooker "kid"), which recalls

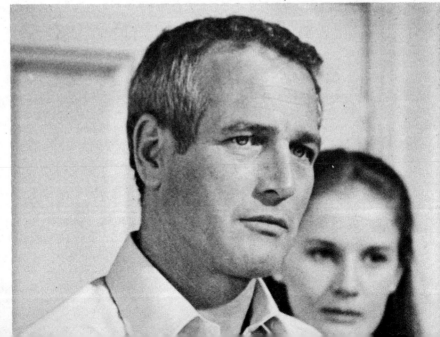

THE MACKINTOSH MAN (1973). With Dominique Sanda.

THE STING (1973). With Robert Redford.

not so much the Butch-Sundance friendship as the many films in which an older man breaks a novice into a profession. Of course, Newman is too young and Redford too old for such a relationship, but the film is not intended as a meaningful character study that can hold up under analysis.

Both actors are constantly charming, but neither is required to do much serious acting. Newman's underplaying begins to look like posing rather than performing. He does have one lively, rather funny scene—a poker game in which

Gondorff and Lonnegan try to out-cheat each other. To annoy Lonnegan, whom he wants to provoke into a larger swindle, Gondorff pretends to be drunk, speaks crudely, belches, deliberately mispronounces his opponent's name, and wipes his nose with a necktie Lonnegan has given him.

The Sting had a mixed critical reception, but those who liked it were extravagant with praise. The National Board of Review voted it Best Picture of the Year, and it received ten Academy Award nominations— more than any other Newman film.

While it was not a milestone for Newman as an actor, it did re-establish his commercial viability. Perhaps it was the Newman-Redford team that made *The Sting* popular, and Newman alone may have difficulty drawing audiences, but he is still considered one of the few remaining superstars.

It will be interesting to see the direction his career will follow. Newman is now in his fiftieth year, but he still has his extraordinary looks and physique, and, like other Hollywood sex symbols, he may endure as a leading man well into his fifties; his romance with a woman twenty-five years his junior in *The Mackintosh Man* is surely in the Gable-Grant-Cooper tradition. On the other hand, he has always wanted to be a character actor, and if this is forced upon him by age, he may relish the opportunity. *Judge Roy Bean*, in which he is a combination of leading man and character personality, seems a suitable stepping-off point.

One thing is certain. In twenty years of film acting, Newman has become one of the screen's most magnetic stars. Even today the very mention of his name evokes an aura of moody rebelliousness, rugged individualism, cool detachment and, above all, overpowering sex appeal. And he has created more memorable characters than have most actors in much longer periods of time. At least four—the Hustler, Hud, Cool Hand Luke and Butch Cassidy—are so well-known, so indelibly impressed on the public consciousness, that they stand among the immortals of the screen.

BIBLIOGRAPHY

Barthel, Joan. "Paul Newman: 'How I Spent My Summer Vacation.' " *New York Times*, October 22, 1967.

Bean, Robin. "Dean—Ten Years After." *Films and Filming*, October, 1965.

—————"Success Begins at Forty." *Films and Filming*, January, 1966.

Bergen, Candice. "The Cool-Sex Boys." *New York Sunday News*, March 19, 1972.

Crawford, Robert, director. *The Making of "Butch Cassidy and the Sundance Kid."* (Film) 1970.

Cutts, John. "James Goldstone Interviewed." *Films and Filming*, January, 1972.

Eyles, Allen. "The Other Brando." *Films and Filming*, January, 1965.

Ferris, John. "Acting is a Painful Experience." *New York World Telegram and Sun*, September 12, 1959.

Fields, Sidney. "Newman: 'As Sexy as a Piece of Bacon.' " *New York Mirror*, June 12, 1959.

Gelmis, Joseph. *The Film Director as Superstar*. Doubleday and Co., New York, 1971.

Godfrey, Lionel. "Tall When They're Small: The Films of Martin Ritt." *Films and Filming*, August, 1968.

Goldman, William. *Butch Cassidy and the Sundance Kid*. (Screenplay) Bantam Books, New York, 1969.

Gow, Gordon. *Hollywood in the Fifties*. A.S. Barnes & Co., New York, 1971.

————— "Involvement." *Films and Filming*, March, 1973.

Herridge, Frances. "Desperate Hours." *New York Post*, July 18, 1955.

Higham, Charles. "Paul Newman Gets High on Speed." *New York Times*, April 18, 1971.

Hughes, Robert, director. *Arthur Penn (1922-): Themes and Variants.* (Film) 1970

Kael, Pauline. *I Lost It at the Movies.* Bantam Books, New York, 1966.

Kauffmann, Stanley. *A World on Film.* Delta, New York, 1967.

————— *Figures of Light.* Harper & Row, New York, 1971.

Lewis, Grover. "The Redoubtable Mr. Newman." *Rolling Stone,* July 5, 1973.

Lewis, Richard Warren. "Paul Newman Makes a Western." *New York Times Magazine,* November 6, 1966.

Maas, Peter. "Newman Scores a K.O." *Colliers,* July 20, 1956.

McVay, Douglas. "The Best and Worst of Martin Ritt." *Films and Filming,* December, 1964.

Milius, John. *The Life and Times of Judge Roy Bean.* (Screenplay) Bantam Books, New York, 1973.

Morgan, Al. "New Breed of Screen Lover." *Show Business Illustrated,* February, 1962.

Quirk, Lawrence J. *The Films of Paul Newman.* Citadel Press, New York, 1971.

Rigdon, Walter, editor. *The Biographical Encyclopedia of Who's Who of the American Theatre.* James H. Heineman, New York, 1965.

Sarris, Andrew. *Confessions of a Cultist.* Simon & Schuster, New York, 1971.

Scott, Vernon. "Similarity? Paul Newman Resents Marlon Brando Tag." *Newark Evening News,* November 4, 1958.

Sherman, Eric and Rubin, Martin. *The Director's Event.* Atheneum, New York, 1970.

Thomas, Tony. *Ustinov in Focus.* A. S. Barnes & Co., New York, 1971.

Truffaut, François. *Hitchcock.* Simon & Schuster, New York, 1967.

Walker, Alexander. *Stardom, The Hollywood Phenomenon.* Stein & Day, New York, 1970.

Wilson, Earl. "Popcorn, Beer and Pop." *New York Post,* May 3, 1959.

Wilson, Jane. "What If My Eyes Turn Brown?" *Saturday Evening Post,* February 24, 1968.

Wood, Robin. *Arthur Penn.* Praeger, Inc., New York, 1970.

————— *Hitchcock's Films.* Paperback Library, New York, 1970.

THE FILMS OF PAUL NEWMAN

The director's name follows the release date. A (c) following the release date indicates that the film is in color. Sp indicates Screenplay and b/o indicates based/on.

1. THE SILVER CHALICE. Warner Brothers, 1954. (c) *Victor Saville.* Sp: Lesser Samuels, b/o novel by Thomas B. Costain. Cast: Virginia Mayo, Pier Angeli, Walter Hampden, Joseph Wiseman, Alexander Scourby, Lorne Greene, E.G. Marshall, Natalie Wood.

2. THE RACK. MGM, 1956. *Arnold Laven.* Sp: Stewart Stern, b/o television play by Rod Serling. Cast: Wendell Corey, Walter Pidgeon, Edmond O'Brien, Anne Francis, Lee Marvin, Cloris Leachman.

3. SOMEBODY UP THERE LIKES ME. MGM, 1956. *Robert Wise.* Sp: Ernest Lehman, b/o autobiography of Rocky Graziano, written with Rowland Barber. Cast: Pier Angeli, Everett Sloane, Eileen Heckart, Sal Mineo, Harold J. Stone.

4. THE HELEN MORGAN STORY. Warner Brothers, 1957. *Michael Curtiz.* Sp: Oscar Saul, Dean Riesner, Stephen Longstreet & Nelson Gidding. Cast: Ann Blyth, Richard Carlson, Gene Evans, Cara Williams, Alan King.

5. UNTIL THEY SAIL. MGM, 1957. *Robert Wise.* Sp: Robert Anderson, b/o story by James Michener. Cast: Jean Simmons, Joan Fontaine, Piper Laurie, Sandra Dee, Charles Drake.

6. THE LEFT-HANDED GUN. Warner Brothers, 1958. *Arthur Penn.* Sp: Leslie Stevens, b/o television play *The Death of Billy the Kid* by Gore Vidal. Cast: Lita Milan, John Dehner, Hurd Hatfield, James Congdon, James Best, Colin Keith-Johnston.

7. THE LONG HOT SUMMER. 20th Century-Fox, 1958. (c) *Martin Ritt.* Sp: Irving Ravetch & Harriet Frank, Jr., b/o stories *Barn Burning* & *The Spotted Horses* & novel *The Hamlet,* all by William Faulkner. Cast: Joanne Woodward, Anthony Franciosa, Orson Welles, Lee Remick, Angela Lansbury, Richard Anderson, Sarah Marshall.

8. CAT ON A HOT TIN ROOF. MGM, 1958. (c) *Richard Brooks.* Sp: Richard Brooks & James Poe, b/o play by Tennessee Williams. Cast: Elizabeth Taylor, Burl Ives, Jack Carson, Judith Anderson, Madeleine Sherwood.

9. RALLY 'ROUND THE FLAG, BOYS! 20th Century-Fox, 1958. (c) *Leo McCarey.* Sp: Claude Binyon & Leo McCarey, b/o novel by Max Shulman. Cast: Joanne Woodward, Joan Collins, Jack Carson, Dwayne Hickman, Tuesday Weld, Gale Gordon.

10. THE YOUNG PHILADELPHIANS. Warner Brothers, 1959. *Vincent Sherman.* Sp: James Gunn, b/o novel *The Philadelphian* by Richard Powell. Cast: Barbara Rush, Diane Brewster, Brian Keith, Alexis Smith, Billie Burke, Robert Vaughn.

11. FROM THE TERRACE. 20th Century-Fox, 1960. (c) *Mark Robson.* Sp: Ernest Lehman, b/o novel by John O'Hara. Cast: Joanne Woodward, Myrna Loy, Ina Balin, Leon Ames, George Grizzard, Patrick O'Neal, Barbara Eden.

12. EXODUS. United Artists, 1960. (c) *Otto Preminger.* Sp: Dalton Trumbo, b/o novel by Leon Uris. Cast: Eva Marie Saint, Ralph Richardson, Peter Lawford, Lee J. Cobb, Sal Mineo, John Derek, Hugh Griffith, David Opatoshu, Jill Haworth.

13. THE HUSTLER. 20th Century-Fox, 1961. *Robert Rossen.* Sp: Robert Rossen & Sidney Carroll, b/o novel by Walter Tevis. Cast: Jackie Gleason, Piper Laurie, George C. Scott, Myron McCormick, Murray Hamilton, Michael Constantine.

14. PARIS BLUES. United Artists, 1961. *Martin Ritt.* Sp: Jack Sher, Irene Kamp & Walter Bernstein; adaptation: Lulla Adler, b/o novel by Harold Flender. Cast: Joanne Woodward, Sidney Poitier, Louis Armstrong, Diahann Carroll, Serge Reggiani, Barbara Laage.

15. SWEET BIRD OF YOUTH. MGM, 1962. (c) *Richard Brooks.* Sp: Richard Brooks, b/o play by Tennessee Williams. Cast: Geraldine Page, Shirley Knight, Ed Begley, Rip Torn, Mildred Dunnock, Madeleine Sherwood.

16. HEMINGWAY'S ADVENTURES OF A YOUNG MAN. 20th Century-Fox, 1962. (c) *Martin Ritt*. Sp: A.E. Hotchner, b/o stories by Ernest Hemingway. Cast: Richard Beymer, Diane Baker, Corinne Calvet, Fred Clark, Dan Dailey, James Dunn, Juano Hernandez, Ricardo Montalban, Susan Strasberg, Jessica Tandy, Eli Wallach.

17. HUD. Paramount, 1963. *Martin Ritt*. Sp: Irving Ravetch & Harriet Frank, Jr., b/o novel *Horseman, Pass By* by Larry McMurtry. Cast: Melvyn Douglas, Patricia Neal, Brandon de Wilde, John Ashley, Whit Bissell.

18. A NEW KIND OF LOVE. Paramount, 1963. (c) *Melville Shavelson*. Sp: Melville Shavelson. Cast: Joanne Woodward, Thelma Ritter, Eva Gabor, George Tobias, Marvin Kaplan, Robert Clary, Maurice Chevalier.

19. THE PRIZE. MGM, 1964. (c) *Mark Robson*. Sp: Ernest Lehman, b/o novel by Irving Wallace. Cast: Edward G. Robinson, Elke Sommer, Diane Baker, Micheline Presle, Gerard Oury, Sergio Fantoni, Kevin McCarthy, Leo G. Carroll.

20. WHAT A WAY TO GO! 20th Century-Fox, 1964 (c) *J. Lee Thompson*. Sp: Betty Comden & Adolph Green, b/o story by Gwen Davis. Cast: Shirley MacLaine, Robert Mitchum, Dean Martin, Gene Kelly, Bob Cummings, Dick Van Dyke, Reginald Gardiner, Margaret Dumont.

21. THE OUTRAGE. MGM, 1964. *Martin Ritt*. Sp: Michael Kanin, b/o film *Rashomon* by Akira Kurosawa and play *Rashomon* by Fay & Michael Kanin. Cast: Laurence Harvey, Claire Bloom, Edward G. Robinson, William Shatner, Howard da Silva, Albert Salmi.

22. LADY L. MGM, 1966. (c) *Peter Ustinov*. Sp: Peter Ustinov, b/o novel by Romain Gary. Cast: Sophia Loren, David Niven, Cecil Parker, Marcel Dalio, Phillipe Noiret, Michel Piccoli, Peter Ustinov.

23. HARPER. Warner Brothers, 1966. (c) *Jack Smight*. Sp: William Goldman, b/o novel *The Moving Target* by Ross MacDonald. Cast: Lauren Bacall, Julie Harris, Arthur Hill, Janet Leigh, Pamela Tiffin, Robert Wagner, Robert Webber, Shelley Winters, Strother Martin.

24. TORN CURTAIN. Universal, 1966. (c) *Alfred Hitchcock*. Sp: Brian Moore. Cast: Julie Andrews, Lila Kedrova, Hansjoerg Felmy, Wolfgang Kieling, Tamara Toumanova, Gunther Strack, Ludwig Donath, David Opatoshu.

25. HOMBRE. 20th Century-Fox, 1967. (c) *Martin Ritt*. Sp: Irving Ravetch & Harriet Frank, Jr., b/o novel by Elmore Leonard. Cast: Fredric March, Richard Boone, Diane Cilento, Cameron Mitchell, Barbara Rush, Peter Lazer, Margaret Blye, Martin Balsam.

26. COOL HAND LUKE. Warner Brothers, 1967. (c) *Stuart Rosenberg*. Sp: Donn Pearce & Frank R. Pierson, b/o novel by Pearce. Cast: George Kennedy, J.D. Cannon, Lou Antonio, Robert Drivas, Strother Martin, Jo Van Fleet, Dennis Hopper.

27. THE SECRET WAR OF HARRY FRIGG. Universal, 1968. (c) *Jack Smight*. Sp: Peter Stone & Frank Tarloff, b/o story by Tarloff. Cast: Sylva Koscina, Andrew Duggan, Tom Bosley, John Williams, Charles D. Gray, Vito Scotti, Jacques Roux, Werner Peters, James Gregory.

28. WINNING. Universal, 1969. (c) *James Goldstone*. Sp: Howard Rodman. Cast: Joanne Woodward, Richard Thomas, Robert Wagner, David Sheiner, Clu Gulager.

29. BUTCH CASSIDY AND THE SUNDANCE KID. 20th Century-Fox, 1969. (c) *George Roy Hill*. Sp: William Goldman. Cast: Robert Redford, Katharine Ross, Strother Martin, Henry Jones, Jeff Corey, George Furth, Cloris Leachman, Ted Cassidy, Kenneth Mars.

30. WUSA. Paramount, 1970. (c) *Stuart Rosenberg*. Sp: Robert Stone, b/o his novel *Hall of Mirrors*. Cast: Joanne Woodward, Anthony Perkins, Laurence Harvey, Pat Hingle, Cloris Leachman, Don Gordon, Michael Anderson, Jr., Leigh French, Moses Gunn, Bruce Cabot.

31. SOMETIMES A GREAT NOTION. Universal, 1971. (c) *Paul Newman*. Sp: John Gay, b/o novel by Ken Kesey. Cast: Henry Fonda, Lee Remick, Michael Sarrazin, Richard Jaeckel, Linda Lawson, Cliff Potts.

32. POCKET MONEY. National General, 1972. (c) *Stuart Rosenberg*. Sp: Terry Malick, b/o novel *Jim Kane* by J.P.S. Brown. Cast: Lee Marvin, Strother Martin, Christine Belford, Kelly Jean Peters, Fred Graham, Wayne Rogers.

33. THE LIFE AND TIMES OF JUDGE ROY BEAN. National General, 1972. (c) *John Huston*. Sp: John Milius. Cast: Jacqueline Bisset, Tab Hunter, John Huston, Stacy Keach, Roddy McDowall, Anthony Perkins, Victoria Principal, Anthony Zerbe, Ava Gardner.

34. THE MACKINTOSH MAN. Warner Brothers, 1973. (c) *John Huston*. Sp: Walter Hill, b/o novel *The Freedom Trap* by Desmond Bagley. Cast: Dominique Sanda, James Mason, Harry Andrews, Ian Bannen, Michael Hordern, Nigel Patrick.

35. THE STING. Universal, 1973. (c) *George Roy Hill*. Sp: David S. Ward. Cast: Robert Redford, Robert Shaw, Charles Durning, Ray Walston, Robert Earl Jones, John Heffernan, Eileen Brennan.

FILMS DIRECTED BY PAUL NEWMAN

1. ON THE HARMFULNESS OF TOBACCO. Kayos Productions (Paul Newman), 1961. Sp: play by Anton Chekhov. Cast: Michael Strong.

2. RACHEL, RACHEL. Warner Brothers, 1968. (c) Sp: Stewart Stern, b/o novel *A Jest of God* by Margaret Laurence. Cast: Joanne Woodward, James Olson, Kate Harrington, Estelle Parsons, Geraldine Fitzgerald, Frank Corsaro, Nell Potts.

3. ˇSOMETIMES A GREAT NOTION. Universal, 1971. (c) Sp: John Gay, b/o novel by Ken Kesey. Cast: Paul Newman, Henry Fonda, Lee Remick, Michael Sarrazin, Richard Jaeckel, Linda Lawson, Cliff Potts.

4. THE EFFECT OF GAMMA RAYS ON MAN-IN-THE-MOON MARIGOLDS. 20th Century-Fox, 1972. (c) Sp: Alvin Sargent, b/o play by Paul Zindel. Cast: Joanne Woodward, Nell Potts, Roberta Wallach, Judith Lowry.

STAGE APPEARANCES BY PAUL NEWMAN

1. PICNIC. 1953-54. *Joshua Logan*. By William Inge. Cast: Ralph Meeker, Janice Rule, Kim Stanley, Eileen Heckart, Arthur O'Connell.

2. THE DESPERATE HOURS. 1955. *Robert Montgomery*. By Joseph Hayes, b/o his novel. Cast: Karl Malden, Nancy Coleman, James Gregory, George Grizzard.

3. SWEET BIRD OF YOUTH. 1959-60. *Elia Kazan*. By Tennessee Williams. Cast: Geraldine Page, Sidney Blackmer, Rip Torn, Madeleine Sherwood, Diana Hyland, Bruce Dern.

4. BABY WANT A KISS. 1964. *Frank Corsaro*. By James Costigan. Cast: Joanne Woodward, James Costigan.

INDEX